The 'Girl Question' in Education

Studies in Curriculum History Series

General Editor: **Professor Ivor Goodson,** Faculty of Education,
University of Western Ontario, London,
Canada N6G 1G7

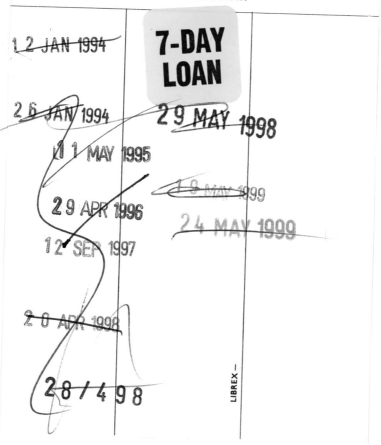

Studies in Curriculum History

The 'Girl Question' in Education

Vocational Education for Young Women in the Progressive Era

Jane Bernard Powers

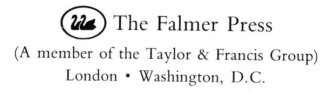 The Falmer Press

(A member of the Taylor & Francis Group)
London • Washington, D.C.

UK   The Falmer Press, 4 John St., London WC1N 2ET
USA   The Falmer Press, Taylor & Francis Inc., 1900 Frost Road, Suite 101,
        Bristol, PA 19007

© Jane Bernard Powers 1992

First published 1992

**A Catalogue Record for this book is available from the British
Library**

ISBN 1 85000 847 7

Library of Congress Cataloguing-in-Publication Data
Powers, Jane Bernard.
  The girl question in education: vocational education for young
women in the progressive era / Jane Bernard Powers.
     p.   cm.—(Studies in curriculum history series)
     Originally presented as the author's thesis (Ph.D.)—Stanford
University, 1987.
  Includes bibliographical references and index.
  ISBN 1–85000–847–7
  1. Women—Vocational education—United States—History.
2. Business education—United States—History.   3. Home
economics—United States—History.   4. Education and state—United
States—History.   I. Title.   II. Series.
LC1503.P68   1992
374'.01'0973—dc20   91–31386
                                                                      CIP

Cover design by Caroline Archer

Typeset in 9.5/11 Bembo
by Graphicraft Typesetters Ltd., Hong Kong

*Printed in Great Britain by Burgess Science Press, Basingstoke
on paper which has a specified pH value on final paper
manufacture of not less than 7·5 and is therefore 'acid free'.*

Contents

Dedication:

For my family

my daughter, Michelle

my sister and brothers,
Sue Ellen, John, and Chuck

and my great-grandmother Johanna
who came from Norway,
went through Ellis Island
and then went into 'the service'.

Acknowledgments

Many projects are accomplished with the help of communities. This is particularly true of this work. I am especially grateful to the communities of scholars and colleagues who by their writing and courage give me heart, ideas to ponder, and encouragement to pursue my own work and ideas.

There are individuals who made significant contributions to the project. David B. Tyack has been sustaining in his interest and encouragement and generous with his ideas and finds. Barrie Franklin was the critic for a small part of the project presented at AERA and since then has been consistently supportive. With characteristic collegial generosity he referred me to Falmer Press. Lynda Stone read the manuscript in various stages and has been an extraordinary critic, colleague and friend.

The librarians and collections at Schlesinger Library, Radcliffe, The Education Library, Vanderbilt University and the Cubberley and Green Libraries, Stanford University, were invaluable.

Sue Verhalen helped the manuscript through final steps on my antiquated word processing system with humor and competence. The Falmer editors do their work with appreciable grace and patience.

Friends and family have been very generous and understanding. I am especially grateful to Toby Bernstein, Richard Bernstein, Jeannette Hebbert, Michael Wheale, Nancy Martin, Pat Gallagher, Carol Langbort, Kay Mills and Michelle who now understands why we have to do 'our work'. I thank you all.

List of Plates

All photographs are reproduced courtesy of the Library of Congress, Photo Archives Department. They are located in the Frances Benjamin Johnston Collection, New York City Schools Collection, Vocational Training for Women (National Training School for Women and Girls) and miscellaneous photographs of boys and girls learning trades in schools.

Cover
Girls learning breadmaking in their home economics class. Boston Schools circa. 1909 Lewis W. Hine Photo, Courtesy of the Library of Congress.

Plates 1 and 2
Laundry room and the laundry building at the National Training School for Women and Girls in Washington, DC.

Plate 3
Working girls and women in Evening Schools, Boston, MA, circa. 1915.

Plate 4
Young women in a home economics class, Washington, DC Schools circa. 1900. The photograph was shown at the 1900 Paris Exhibition. Frances Benjamin Johnston Collection, courtesy of the Library of Congress.

Plate 5
'Making Dollar Dresses at Washington Irving High School', New York City Schools, courtesy of the Library of Congress.

Plate 6
Young women learning stenography at the National Training School for Women and Girls in Washington, DC, circa. 1925, courtesy of the Library of Congress.

Introduction

David B. Tyack

At the beginning of the twentieth century, many Americans were bedevilled by what they called 'the boy problem' in education. Basically, the boy problem was that boys did not do as well in school as girls. They repeated grades more often, received lower grades, were more rebellious, and 'dropped out' in droves (the term itself was coined about 1900 by educators). A favored solution at the time was to create a new kind of education for these students: vocational training that would engage the interests and talents of 'hand-minded' boys. Thus from the beginning, vocational education was touted as a way to make schooling more masculine.

With few exceptions, historians of vocationalism have followed the lead of the pioneers in the field by neglecting girls. But now in this insightful and important book, Jane Bernard Powers illuminates the other side of the story, the vocational education of girls. She roots her analysis in the larger issues raised by what contemporaries called 'the woman question', or, as one observer put it, 'What ought woman to be?'. Debates over how schools should prepare young women for their future lives became a stage for far-ranging disputes over gender relationships in the larger society, not simply pedagogical arguments. In discussing home economics Americans sought to arrest a perceived decline in the family, and in prescribing new forms of trade education, some tried to correct the gender inequalities of corporate capitalism.

But Powers does not analyze only competing ideologies. She also juxtaposes prescriptions to politics and practices in vocational education. She restores to their rightful place in history a fascinating cast of women actors in the movement who developed and lobbied for vocational education of many different stripes. Here are the clubwomen who testified before Congress or local school boards for programs in home economics, and militant trade union women who argued for equal opportunities for female blue collar workers. She shows that it is a false dichotomy to think of such activists as either feminist or traditional in their views of women's destiny, for such categories are ends of a spectrum, not a forced choice. Here are not passive victims of male domination but women who actively shaped policy and carried out a variety of different programs.

In examining practice Powers draws on a wide variety of sources to demonstrate the quite different fates of various types of vocational training. Home economics, she argues, never came close to fulfilling the grandiose claims of its more flamboyant proponents. Hopes of social salvation became transformed into making white sauce, stitching seams, and doing the laundry. When given a choice, girls mostly elected other subjects. Powers documents that educators used home economics as one vehicle of class and racial stratification.

Although radical women trade unionists hoped to build, through education, ladders of skill and responsibility that women could climb within the workforce, opposition from unions and employers, and other educators sabotaged the plan. A girl might enter the factory at the age of forty. Parents and students, thinking that high schools should lead to white collar jobs, steered clear of training that led to blue collar jobs.

Powers shows that the success in the shadows was commercial education. Few millennial claims were made for business training, but it did prepare young women for jobs they wanted, albeit on an echelon that has been called 'pink collar'. Most of the rhetoric about vocational education and the federal Smith-Hughes Act of 1917 neglected business education; it seemed too middle class, too academic, and too female to occupy the attention of the male oriented social reformers. But girls and their parents thought commercial education a pathway into respectable, even romantic, jobs, especially when compared to factory work. And employers, loathe to spend time and money for on-the-job training for young women (whom they assumed to be temporary workers), readily hired female high school graduates as secretaries and clerks in the rapidly expanding tertiary sector of the economy.

Now that people again debate the 'woman question' in the form of equal opportunity for women, Powers's book is a timely and significant contribution to the literature of educational history and women's history.

1 Beginnings

Reform and progress were watchwords of the day in the early twentieth century, and they were synonymous with the Progressive Era in the United States.[1] The vocational education movement was harnessed to both, and like many educational reform movements that followed, it was full of promise in the birthing. Helen and Robert Lynd reported in their landmark study of middle America that vocational training had become the 'darling of Middletown's eye'.[2] Vocational education was destined, at the very least, to change the face of curriculum in junior and senior high schools.

All young people could benefit from this educational reform, the advocates argued, however some would benefit more than others. Ethnically diverse adolescents who dropped out of school well before graduation were a special target population. As Helen Todd, a factory inspector in Chicago, found in her interviews with children in factories, many preferred factory work to the harsh conditions of urban schools.[3] Faced with high dropout rates, pressure from industrial and corporate leaders who looked to schools for a disciplined and productive labor force, and a genuine compassion for the poverty experienced by urban families, educators banded together with industrialists and social reformers to improve the vocational destinies of young people. They believed that the 'deleterious effects' of industrialization and urbanization would be alleviated and agrarian and industrial productivity increased if Greek, Latin, and other irrelevancies in education were drummed out or minimized in favor of more practical subjects and programs. According to the popular vision, students were to be educated according to their presumed life chances or their 'vocational destinies'.[4]

Although the movement successfully united a diverse group of influential supporters including David Snedden, Commissioner of Education in Massachusetts, Jane Addams the noted domestic feminist and founder of Hull House Settlement in Chicago, and President Theodore Roosevelt, who represented agrarian interests in the crusade, it had both critics and conflicts. Some argued that schools would become factories that produced young workers, while others forecast the dominance of schools by manufacturing and industrial interests. School people worried that class divisions and inequities would result if vocational education was separated from the comprehensive high school curriculum.

While debates over who should control vocational schooling and how it should be structured engaged schoolmen, politicians, and social reformers, an equally profound set of issues emerged in discussions about the vocational destiny of young women. Women's visibly increased presence in the work place disturbed the myth that a woman's place was the home: woman's place was now both a question and a problem. Society generally and schools specifically argued about the purposes of women's education. Should schools provide training for young women who will be employed outside the home or for 'functional needs of the major group of girls who will be homemakers'?[5]

The 'girl question' in education emerged from the 'woman question' which was a lively and intense argument over women's economic, political, and social roles and their psychological, intellectual, and physical capabilities. The 'woman question,' which extended across North America, Great Britain, and the Continent, has been characterized by contemporary historians as both a critique of western patriarchy and a central political concern of the late nineteenth and early twentieth centuries.[6]

The seeds of the 'woman question', planted in the nineteenth century, blossomed into a full scale debate in the early twentieth century. The controversy over the role of women in the United States was like a rapidly growing young tree with roots that sprang from and crossed over many issues. These included suffrage, economic independence, the perceived demise of the home, and general demands for equity. The general discussion of a woman's place became part and parcel of the women's vocational training movement.

The spectrum of opinion on the 'girl question' in vocational training was as wide and diverse as the spectrum of opinions on the role of women generally, and as complex as feminism was during this period. Some people favored an exclusive emphasis on home economics; a vocal minority lobbied for an exclusive emphasis on training for industry; many others supported compromise positions. Other factors such as class, race, and urban–rural differences added to the diversity of opinion on appropriate vocational training programs for young women.

Significantly, the United States was not alone in the emergence of prescriptions for girls' and women's education. Differentiated education was a subject that stretched across oceans and continents, but in each setting the form and arguments were shaped by the particular context. State controlled schools in both Great Britain and Australia were pressured to adopt domestic science as a mainstay of female education.[7] Moreover, arguments about race suicide that surfaced in the United States were also used to justify a woman's curriculum in Great Britain. Dropping birthrates and marriage rates among middle class women, coincident with increased levels of education, became the basis for policy statements connecting race and national efficiency to the teaching of domestic science.

The vocational education movement in the United States marked a turning point in public education for young women, when sex segregation and the treatment of women based on their special characteristics and needs became a formal agenda of public schools. This book is about the genesis and development of the vocational education movement for young women in the United States during the years 1900 to 1930.

Much of the historical work on vocational education written in the seventies and early eighties focused on the qualities and dynamics of the schooling work nexus as an outgrowth of the liberal vocational debate. Revisionist histories of the means and structures for reproducing a segmented hierarchical labor force in schools prompted critiques that argued for more inclusive histories that consider gender, ethnicity, and regional contexts along with class. Kantor and Tyack's edited book, (1982) *Work, Youth and Schooling*, and Kantor's book (1987) *Learning to Earn*, provide examples of histories that broadened the scope of issues to include 'perspectives on changing contexts, attitudes, and institutions ...' *Work, Youth and Schooling* includes an excellent essay entitled, 'Marry, Stitch, Die or Do Worse', by Clifford, and *Learning to Earn* includes brief segments on the implications of vocational education for young women.[8] Relying primarily on state and federal documents and early writings on vocational education, including periodicals and California media sources, Kantor focuses on the successes and failures of vocational education in strengthening the connections between schooling and work. Comments on the significance of the movement for women is not a major focus of this work which proceeds from the 'boy question' in education. Rury's work enriched the historical picture by focusing on women in his analyses of the connections between labor markets and schooling for women.[9]

The Girl Question complements prior work by moving questions of gender and women from the margins to the spotlight and by telling the story from the perspective of women. Using data from state and national government sources, feminine and feminist organizational proceedings and publications, and private papers of women such as Margaret Dreier Robins, this work considers the vocational movement from the perspective of women and girls. The diverse positions of advocates such as trade unionists, program developers such as home economists, and students who filled typing classes and boycotted home economics are illuminated by the dynamic social, economic, and political context of the early twentieth century in the United States. This historical work focuses on multiple perspectives and meanings rather than building a unified argument.

Thus, an early question that motivated this work, was home economics in public school an instrument of social and economic control?, was abandoned for its simplicity and narrowness. Broader themes and issues, central to progressive-era feminism emerged from the margins of vocational education politics and history to reveal a loosely structured but developed campaign for women's education. This campaign for women's vocational education exposed and challenged essential understandings about the purposes of education for young men and young women. Thus it was both a social and an educational movement.

The story of the vocational education movement for women is in part about the Progressive Era women's movement and the diverse opinions women held about the path they needed to clear and defend to ensure their role in the mainstream of modern industrial society. It is also about the need to create policies governing and defining women's vocational programs and the political forces and organizational politics that were brought to that process. The third dimension is about the power of students, parents, and educators to negotiate, resist, and shape the prescriptions and the policies.[10] Each section is like a separate picture of the same subject, taken from different angles and using a different lens. Together the complexity of the pattern, the differences in race, class, rural, urban, and feminine/feminist strategies, and politics emerge under the umbrella of gender.

The cross fertilization of women's history, women's educational history, and contemporary education history has provided the conceptual tools that illuminate and explain this history. The first tool or lens provides the general lighting for the other more specific historical themes. It is the notion that historical understanding is best served by avoiding seamless pre-existing categories and arguments that are mutually exclusive and tightly bounded. As Joan Scott has argued about feminist theory, 'We need theory that will let us think in terms of pluralities and diversities rather than of unities and universals'.[11] In the context of the 'girl question', it is important to view feminism and traditionalism as fluid categories that represent connected experiences. Home economics is both traditional and feminist, it contains continuities and contradictions. For women, the vocational education movement and programatic outcomes were at once constraining and liberating and the quality of these varied according to the particularity of class, ethnicity, and race in context. The three more specific lenses that frame this history are cultural context, myth and reality, and the relationship between traditional and progressive values and attitudes in an era of change. Cultural context plays a significant part in this study of women's vocational education which explains vocational education in its elaborate, intricate, involvement with the rest of society.[12] The history of women's vocational training is very much a product of the Progressive Era and the attempts of women – both individually and within organizations – to define themselves in relation to the family and the workplace and to establish their place in what promised to be a new age. What were the specific Progressive Era issues and themes that influenced discussions and decisions regarding women's vocational training? How was the movement influenced by women's individual and organizational response to these issues? These are the contextual questions addressed in this historical study.

Distinguishing between myth and reality and identifying the relationship between the two is a facet of all historians' work. The relationship between myth and reality is particularly important in the history of vocational training for women because the rhetoric of the movement was so intense, the contrast to reality so great, and the relationship between the two so close. The educational prescriptions advanced by women and their organizations in discussions of women's vocational training reflected both the potence of the myth that woman's place is in the home and its utility in masking women's progress out of the home. Student and parent responses both validated and repudiated the myth of a woman's place, as students negotiated their way through the reality of vocational programs and the narrow choices in the labor market. Thus the broad question proposed by this theme is, what was the relationship between myth and reality, and how did it influence prescriptions, program, and practice?

The third major theme is the paradoxical relationship of feminism and traditionalism. The range of opinions, the policies developed, and the programs established can not be understood if they are viewed as either traditional or feminist because they were often both at once; traditional and feminist values, attitudes, and behavior co-existed. Neither were those who supported and defended home economics monolithically traditionalists, nor were the trade education supporters uniformly feminist or politically liberal. The question that emerges from this theme is, how did the intersecting currents of traditional and feminist values and perspectives influence the prescriptive messages articulated by women's organizations, educators, and social commentators in the policy discussions that preceded legislation and course offerings in schools?

The essential argument in this work is that the key issues and influences in the vocational education movement for young women were not primarily economic, they were a broad canvas of social, political, and economic forces that were shaped by specific contexts. The primary purpose of this book is to provide multiple 'ways of seeing' this movement in women's educational history so that the richness and complexity of curricular change as social movement is illuminated.[13]

Notes

1 The Progressive Era in the United States generally refers to the years between 1880 and 1920 which gave rise to the Progressive political party, support for women's suffrage and a host of social and political reform issues.

2 Lynd, R. and H. (1956 reprint of 1929 edition) *Middletown*, New York, Harcourt, Brace and World Inc., p. 195.

3 Todd, H. (1913) 'Why Children Work: The Children's Answer', *McClures Magazine*, 40, pp. 68–79 in Kantor, H. and Tyack, D.B. (Eds) *Work, Youth, and Schooling, Historical Perspectives on Vocationalism in American Education*, Stanford, Stanford University Press, p. 30.

4 See Kantor, H. and Tyack, D.B. (1982) *Work, Youth, and Schooling, Historical Perspectives on Vocationalism in American Education*, for work on the history of vocational education.

5 Lynd, R. and H. (1956 reprint of 1929 edition) *Middletown*, New York, Harcourt, Brace and World Inc., p. 198.

6 For discussion of the 'woman question' and references see Rothman, S. (1978) *Woman's Proper Place*, New York, Basic Books; Bell, S.G. and Offen, K.M. (1983) *Women, the Family and Freedom, Volume II, 1880–1950*, Stanford, Stanford University Press, pp. 2–3.

7 Hunt, F. (1987) *Lessons for Life, The Schooling of Girls and Women 1850–1950*, Oxford, Basil Blackwell Ltd, p. 9; Porter, P. (1986) *Sociology of the School, Gender and Education*, Victoria, Deakin University Press, pp. 22–32.

8 Kantor, H. and Tyack, D.B. *Work, Youth and Schooling*; Kantor, H. (1988) *Learning to Earn* Madison, University of Wisconsin Press.

9 Rury, J. (1984) 'Vocationalism for Home and Work: Women's Education in the United States, 1890–1930', *History of Education Quarterly*, 34, pp. 21–45.

10 Anyon, J. (1983) 'Intersections of Gender and Class: Accommodation and Resistance by Working-Class and Affluent Females to Contradictory Sex-Role Ideologies', in Walker, S. and Barton, L. (Eds) *Gender, Class and Education*, Lewes, The Falmer Press, pp. 19–38.

11 Scott, J. (1988) 'Deconstructing Equality-Versus-Difference: or, The Uses of Poststructuralist Theory for Feminism', *Feminist Studies*, 14, 1, p. 33; Rabine, L. (1988) 'A Feminist Politics of Non-Identity', Ibid., pp. 11–25.

12 Bailyn, B. (1960) *Education in the Forming of American Society*, Chapel Hill, University of North Carolina Press, p. 14, quoted in Clifford, G. (1976) 'Education: History and Historiography', *Review of Research in Education*, Washington, DC, American Education Research Association, p. 214.

13 Tyack, D. and Hansot, E. (1982) *Managers of Virtue, Public School Leadership in America, 1820–1980*, New York, Basic Books, p. 12.

Part 1

Prescription and Myth

Part 1 Introduction – Prescription and Myth

Prescriptions are essentially myths that reflect an idealized state of being and that set standards for attitudes and behavior. Elizabeth Janeway has written that myths are 'false in fact and true to human yearnings and ... and thus at all times a powerful shaping force'.[1] For example, the 'cult of true womanhood' in the nineteenth century had more to do with myth than with the reality of women's lives, especially working women.[2] In the context of discussions about vocational education, prescriptions represented the myths about women's roles that individuals and organizations wanted to maintain. For young women prescriptions defined what they were supposed to consider vocationally, not necessarily what they did consider.[3]

In the vocational education movement, discussions about the appropriate content of courses and programs for young women were more symbolic than substantive. They represented the need for mainly middle and upper class women to reconcile nineteenth century ideals and social roles with the challenges of twentieth century life: industrialism, changing political roles for middle class women, and changing opportunities for working class women.

Complicating the discussion from the outset was the problem of women's place. Some people were not sure that the question of vocational training applied to women. After all, they were not going to be the 'captains of industry' and they were not going to furnish labor for the industrial machines that would compete with Germany's growing industrial strength. In a sense women occupied a stepchild status within the vocational movement. Male leaders were ambivalent or opposed to women's role in the work world. Many were not interested in an issue which did not carry a great deal of prestige, and others were reluctant to delve into an issue as sensitive as the 'woman question'.

Alice Kessler-Harris, in her essay, 'Women, Work and the Social Order', characterized the upheaval in this period as a 'tension between the need for labor and the need for social order'.[4] The 'need for labor' grew out of the changing complexion of the work place. The rise of factories and the consolidation of the corporate sector, along with increased mechanization and specialization of tasks, created a place for women in the labor market to perform low paying, low status and seasonal work. Women were welcomed into the market place by employers who found them to be 'more reliable, more easily controlled, cheaper, more temperate, more easily procured, neater, more rapid, more industrious, more careful, more polite, less liable to strike ...'.[5] The inherent contradiction between the market needs and the myth of true womanhood was not reconciled; it was generally ignored. But, the myth of true womanhood stood in the wings of the industrial workplace to be paraded out when it was socially or economically expedient, thus marginalizing women's work.

What is equally important is that women, especially young single women welcomed the chance to work in schools, factories and offices. In 1890 the number of women engaged in manufacturing, mechanical, and clerical jobs was 829,373. By 1910 the figure had swelled to 2,380,914, an increase of almost 200 per cent.[6] The right to work was a major issue in feminism at the turn of the century and while many young women were compelled by circumstance to work and contribute to the family income, many wanted to work and looked forward to economic independence.

There were, however, powerful forces opposing women's growing position in the work force and notable among these were male workers. Women were viewed as competitors who had a depressing effect on the wages of men. One proponent of this theory wrote that, 'The wage bargaining power of men is weakened by the competition of women and children, hence a law restricting the hours of women and children may also be looked upon as a law to protect men in their bargaining powers'.[7] Some men also complained that working in industrial establishments had dangerous effects on women's reproductive capacities; that it was likely to unsex women, and further more that it led to immorality.[8] The general problem was of sufficient importance to critics that in 1894 Congress called upon the Bureau of Labor to investigate the employment of women 'and the effect, if any, upon the wages and employment of men'.[9] When the data were collected researchers reported that 'females are to some extent entering into places at the expense ... of males'.[10] Opposition to the working woman did not diminish over time, and the protests became especially shrill when women assumed the jobs reserved for men during World War I and handily increased production in many areas.

Concerns about the social order were causatively linked to working women. The increasing incidence of working women was linked to higher divorce rates, prostitution, unsupervised children, and the decay of the family, as well as moral degeneration in general. According to critics, mothers were doing a poor job of caring for and nurturing the future generation of working men and they were not educating their daughters for their roles as future homemakers. Vocational education was a potential solution to these dilemmas and many more, argued the most visionary advocates of differentiated curricula.

Domestic feminists and trade education advocates marshalled their arguments and their resources to grapple with the myths and the realities and to shape the future of women's education *vis-a-vis* vocational education. Women were primarily responsible for generating the rhetoric and prescriptions about women's place which had some interesting and significant consequences. For one thing, unlike the men's vocational education movement which produced a handful of spokesmen who were widely quoted, the women's vocational education movement produced *ad hoc* coalitions. There were no grand architects of women's vocational education and the rhetoric as well as the policies and practices reflect the diversity in perspectives and values that attended the Progressive Era women's movement.

This section of the book is about the prescriptive rhetoric and reality that shaped ideas about the appropriate vocational education for young women in home economics, trade education and commercial education.

Notes

1 Janeway, E. (1977) *Man's World, Woman's Place*, New York, Dell Publishing, Inc., p. 7.
2 Kliebard, H. (1990) 'Vocational Education as Symbolic Action: Connecting Schooling With the Workplace', *American Educational Research Journal*, 27, 1, pp. 9–26.
3 Welter, B. (1978) 'The Cult of True Womanhood, 1820–1860', in Gordon, M. (Ed.), *The American Family in Social Historical Perspective*, New York, St. Martin's Press, pp. 313–333.
4 Harris, A.K. (1982) *Out to Work, A History of Wage Earning Women in the United States*, New York, Oxford Press, pp. 25–29.
5 Smuts, R. (1976) *Women and Work in America*, New York, Schocken Books, p. 139.
6 Hill, J. (1929) *Women in Gainful Occupations 1870–1920, Census Monograph 9* Washington, DC., Government Printing Office, reprint edition, (1978) Westport, Connecticut, Greenwood Press, p. 40.
7 Harris, A.K., op. cit., p. 338.
8 Brandeis, L. (1907 reprint) 'Decision of the United States Supreme Court in *Curt Muller* vs *State of Oregon*', New York, National Consumers' League, passim.
9 Smuts, R. op. cit., p. 119.
10 Ibid., p. 119.

2   Home Economics:
A Panacea for Reform

The publication of Catherine Beecher's *Treatise on Domestic Economy* in 1843 signaled the emergence of a 'new' field of study and a major curriculum reform in women's education, the art and science of homemaking.[1] By the end of the first decade in the twentieth century, this new field, alternately called home arts, domestic science and home economics, had developed into an organized effort to feminize women's education in the United States. The AHEA (American Home Economics Association) and the GFWC (General Federation of Women's Clubs) were collaborating to lobby for the inclusion of home economics in school programs at all levels of the public education system – kindergarten through post graduate school.[2] This chapter is about the people and ideas that supported the growth of home economics in the Progressive Era. The basic questions framing this chapter are, why did home economics become a passionate cause, and what did the campaign represent from an educational history perspective?

This early twentieth century drive to put home economics in school programs coincided with perceived revolutionary changes in women's roles: public demonstrations for suffrage; alarming increases in the percentage of women employed outside the home, a disturbing female dominance in high school enrollments, success in higher education, and elevated divorce rates.[3] Even though most young women were in the paid labor force for only a few years, most did not go to school beyond the ninth grade, and the vast majority married; the illusion and spectre of relentless change was disquieting.

Critics began to raise questions about young women's education; not about access which basically had been settled in the late nineteenth century, but about the appropriateness of their academic curriculum. Shouldn't girls be studying subjects that would fit them for their life work? people asked. Arguing that young women's education at all levels should focus on the life goal of homemaking, articles such as 'What Kind of Education is Best Suited for Girls?' and 'Cross-Purposes in Education of Women', appeared in major educational journals.[4] 'Without help from the public school', wrote one educator, 'many of these girls will, in a few years, enter homes of their own, untaught and irresponsible, to assume the most sacred duties without intelligent preparation, and to perpetuate a type of home that is a menace to the health and standards of the community'.[5]

There were critics of homemaking centered vocational curricula as well. One contributor to a 1914 volume of *Atlantic Monthly* severely criticized the system whereby it was assumed that all young girls would be homemakers while boys could pick from any number of occupations. She wrote, 'But why, I beg to ask, does everyone know that the vocation which is sure to delight every girl and in which she is sure to succeed ... is housekeeping and the rearing of children?'. It was fundamentally false, wrote this woman, 'that one half of the human race should be "educated" for one single occupation, while the multitudinous other occupations of civilized life should all be loaded upon the other half'.[6]

Home economics advocates included people who wanted women to retreat to their nineteenth century 'havens' as well as those who favored increased involvement in public political life.[7] The paradox of the home economics campaign and reform was that it was both traditional and feminist at once and that multiple progressive-era causes and divergent perspectives on the 'woman question' were sheltered under its umbrella. If home economics were properly taught in schools, reformers argued, men would be lured from saloons by good food cooked by cheerful wives. Farm women would stay in the country and thus farm conditions would improve. Middle class women's lives would take on new meaning through scientific homemaking and municipal housekeeping. Girls destined for domestic service would be properly trained and the high standards of American homes maintained. Moreover, racial uplift could be achieved for black people. Home economics was a progressive-era panacea for the reform of American society that engaged the attention of a remarkable range of interest groups and personalities and reflected a laundry basket of progressive era issues and themes.[8] Science and business as models, immigration, and the exodus of women from farms were among the issues that fueled domestic science campaigns. Above all else the home economics campaign thrust the issue of education for girls and women into the living room of American people.

And how was this engineered? This early twentieth century lobby for change did not enjoy the benefit of mass media such as television. Instead, the campaign was waged in a variety of settings: in local, state and national meetings of organizations, in board of education meetings, in the growing body of parent schools associations that were springing up around the country, and in living rooms. Newspapers, women's magazines, and women's club bulletins carried the message of reform.

Professional Homemaking: Science, Business and Domestic Feminism

The rise of home economics and its metamorphosis into a major progressive-era feminist cause led to a collaboration between women's organizations and school people to help solve the 'woman question'. The solution to the alleged dilemma of modern women was to professionalize the work of homemakers and to develop schools and curricula which would impart the special knowledge and skills of the profession. Boosters of professional homemaking generally agreed that a woman's place was in the home rather than the work place and that homemaking should be viewed as a profession or a calling. Beyond this agreement, however, there were significant differences among professional homemaking supporters. Ellen Richards emphasized homemaking as a scientific endeavor; Christine Frederick's model of professional homemaking incorporated modern business terminology and technique; and domestic feminists focused on social and political reform aspects of homemaking and housekeeping. All three positions varied in degrees of feminism and traditionalism.

Scientific Housekeeping

One prevalent rationale for home economics was that homemaking and child-rearing were professional pursuits that required study and training. The advent of practical sciences such as nutrition and dietetics, a nascent but growing child study movement and the popularization of scientific management, provided the content and motivation for professional homemaking training. No longer could homemaking be learned as a mother's helper in the kitchen. It became (theoretically) such a complex undertaking that mothers were no longer sufficiently knowledgeable or capable of training daughters for it. As one advocate proclaimed, 'It is no more possible for a woman to manage a household instinctively that for a man to succeed in a business he knows nothing about'.[9]

The professionalization of housework and idealization of domestic science can be traced to Emma Willard and Catharine Beecher who were leading nineteenth century advocates for women's education. Emma Willard legitimized home economics as an area of study when she included 'domestic instruction' in the curriculum plan for the Troy Seminary.[10] While Willard made a significant contribution toward the establishment of home economics as a field of study in schools, it was Catharine Beecher who popularized the field and developed the rationale which would eventually lead to a well developed argument for gender defined curricula and home economics in the secondary school curricula.

Beecher played a significant role in the history of home economics by advocating the idea of a woman's sphere which was based on scientific management of the home and children. She celebrated the science of domestic science in her *Treatise on Domestic Economy*, published in 1841. There she proposed a standardization of American domestic practices and provided guidelines for 'household maintenance, childrearing, gardening, cooking, cleaning, doctoring, and the dozen other responsibilities middle class women assumed ...'.[11]

Beecher's most significant contribution to the home economics movement, apart from categorizing the technology and science of homemaking, was to establish the idea that women had a role to play in society that was separate but equal to men's. In the domestic sphere they could exert their superior moral influence on their families and thereby influence a social circle that extended far beyond the hearth. Beecher was responsible for designing an 'ideology that gave women a central place in national life'. According to historian Kathryn Kish Sklar, Beecher defined a strong feminist position based on the differences between men and women, rather than on their similarities or 'human equality'. Beecher's approach to home economics was thus a combination of traditional values – home and family – and a variant of feminist ideology. Her ideas on domestic economy informed the developing home economics movement and influenced leaders such as Ellen Swallow Richards. Richards was a researcher and teacher who was trained as a chemist at the Massachusetts Institute of Technology. Her interest in the application of chemistry to practical problems such as nutrition, clean air and clean water, led her to home economics where she did research to broaden the scientific basis of home economics, and where she lobbied for more and better home economics in school curriculum.[12]

Richards subscribed to Beecher's theory that women had a separate and equal sphere of responsibilities in life that required a special education. She also believed that the 'lot' of her sex needed to be improved because the productive functions had left the household and women's role had lost much of its meaning. Domestic education was her prescription for this dilemma and this meant education in the appropriate sciences – chemistry, biology and physics – with a major emphasis on practical applications to home problems.[13] Richards mobilized support for her perspective among her expanding army of followers in the AHEA. She and her supporters worked for the inclusion of home economics at all levels of education, kindergarten to college, and she worked for the establishment of science based home economics curricula.

Captains of the Kitchen Adopt Management Skills

Whereas Ellen Richards focused on the science of home economics, Christine Frederick applied business and industrial language and technique to homemaking. Homes were to be thought of as businesses, and homemaking as a management problem that involved knowledge of budgeting and finance, task analysis skills and the ability to look at an entire matrix of household tasks as a management system. Frederick espoused the ideas and methods of Frederick Winslow Taylor, the celebrated captain of industrial efficiency who devised time/motion studies to maximize production in industry.[14]

Frederick adapted time/motion study techniques to homemaking in order to create kitchens that were models of efficiency and productivity, and professional homemakers who were like the captains of industry. For example, she analyzed the motions involved in peeling potatoes which, she said, would consume less than two minutes not counting actual peeling time:

1   Walk to shelf adjacent to sink and get pot.
2   Walk to storage, carrying pot, and fill it with potatoes.
3   Return from storage, laying pot directly on vegetable preparing surface near sink.
4   Pick up knife (from nail above this surface).
5   Pare potatoes directly into pail (soiling no surface).
6   Wash potatoes and fill pot with water.
7   Wash and hang up knife (on nail above sink).
8   Walk with pot and lay on stove.[15]

Frederick believed that scientific management would bring 'industrial efficiency' into the home, thereby dignifying home economics as a management science.[16] She argued that there could be 'applied science' for women as well as for men, and that the laws of heat could be tested by the management of a kitchen stove.

Frederick and her followers believed that the application of science and business principles to home management would revitalize homemaking as a profession and influence daughters to avoid the 'unnatural craving for careers' which was taking women away from their essential responsibilities.[17] Referring to employed women as her enemies, Frederick maintained a very traditional view of women's roles. She did not advocate efficiency in the interest of freeing up time for the pursuit of activities outside the home; she suggested that women use their spare time to read a book or do a project in their homes. Thus Frederick espoused a modernized and professionalized version of the 'true woman', mixing traditional ideals and modern technology in her curious rationale for home economics in the schools.

Science and business rationality were two progressive-era ideals that influenced the campaign for teaching home economics in schools. As the principal of Public School No. 6 in Manhattan wrote, 'It is not thrift in the home, but the scientific management of the home that I want you to teach the children'.[18] By applying science and business to home economics, advocates sought to meld mainstream cultural trends and ideals with women's sphere – thereby elevating the status of women's work and ultimately the power of women, theoretically, while maintaining the boundaries of separate roles. Ultimately this separate but equal approach rationalized sex segregation in secondary schools and promoted training for non-renumerative occupations in a society where an increasing number of women worked outside the home. Moreover, this philosophy may have contributed to the dilution of science courses for women, and ultimately to the drop in female enrollments in science courses during the first two decades of the twentieth century.[19]

Domestic Feminism and Family Protection

Domestic feminists were women who embraced the idea of a woman's sphere centered on home and family responsibilities but wanted the parameters of the sphere expanded to include public institutions.[20] Modern industrial society, according to domestic feminists such as Jane Addams, had forced home functions and responsibilities out into the community.[21] Preservation and protection of women's sphere necessitated following these traditionally home based concerns out into the community and market-place. 'The home going forth into the world', as Frances Willard captioned it, meant that domestic feminist interests would include environmental concerns such as pure air, water, and food; social issues such as protective labor legislation for women and children; and education issues such as home economics and industrial training for working class children.[22]

Women needed a special education that home economics would provide; not only because homemaking was a profession demanding special skill and knowledge, but also because women had to be socialized and trained for their role as municipal housekeepers. Leadership in municipal reform issues such as clean water required knowledge of bacteriology and an understanding of local government functioning. Schools were the logical agencies and home economics the logical program for teaching young women the fundamentals of municipal housekeeping.

The women of the GFWC and the AHEA constituted the critical core of domestic feminists. They were white, middle class women who wanted public power and influence but who eschewed Charlotte Perkins Gilman's belief that economic independence was the key to power for women.[23] Instead the women of the GFWC and the AHEA vied for political power and influence by rejecting suffrage and shrouding the non-traditional caste of their public role under the justification of domesticity. As one woman expressed it in *The Journal of Home Economics*, 'Our ideal woman of today has the house-motherly instinct of the past, trained and disciplined, broadened in scope, deepened in power, penetrated with an even more enduring and subtle charm, and she brings this, not in a strident demand for rights, but as her contribution to the upbuilding of the nation's life'.[24]

Domestic feminists predicated many of their social programs and municipal reform efforts on the importance of women's protective instincts, especially where the family was concerned. Protecting families threatened by urbanization and industrialization, became a major rationale for supporting the teaching of home economics in the schools. Home economics was the agency through which the 'renovation of the home', and salvation of the American family would be accomplished. As one educator expressed it, 'I am steadily growing to believe the future stability of our Republic is almost dependent upon it, so complex has our civilization become and so largely have the homes been neglected ...'.[25]

Domestic feminists were concerned about a number of issues related to family welfare including, divorce, money management, declining birth rates, infant mortality and the health of industrial workers. Divorce was frequently mentioned as both a threat to and an index of the health and stability of family life. The number of divorces granted in the United States per 1,000 existing marriages jumped from 1.2 in 1860 to 7.7 in 1920, thus precipitating grave concern about the stability of the social order.[26] Rheta Child Dorr called the divorce rate, 'the most important social fact we have had to face since the slavery question was settled'.[27] The reasons cited for the increases in the divorce rate varied. Suffragists and militant feminists pointed to women's revolt against intolerable unions as the major cause. More conservative women and men blamed the divorce rate on women's inability to make men happy. According to a noted sociologist, slack conditions in the homes of employed women lead to unsteady and delinquent husbands.[28] Bad homemaking leads men to saloons, and presumably away from marriage, stated another critic.[29]

Senator Carroll Page (R. Vermont), an ardent defender of home economics, argued in Congressional hearings that 'the country is fast awakening to the fact that probably 50 per cent of all divorce would have been avoided had the girls been good cooks, good homemakers, and good mothers'. His solution, and that of many of his contemporaries, was to teach young women how to prepare a tasty and nutritious meal, how to decorate and maintain a house so that homes could compete successfully with the lavish decor of pubs, and how to care for children. 'We must train our girls for homemaking', declared Senator Page, 'for if we do not and if race suicide and divorce continue to increase ... our social conditions will become unbearable'.[30] Contemporaries of Page such as sociologist Edward Ross agreed that 'instruction of girls in domestic science and house-keeping', was a viable remedy for divorce.[31]

Two other related problems that were viewed as serious threats to the well being of the family were declining birth rates and infant mortality rates. Statistical evidence showed that the birthrate among educated peoples was dropping while the birthrate among the 'least promising' sectors was increasing. Critics charged that the root of the 'race suicide' problem – declining birth rates among well born young women – was education for vocations. Young women were being educated away from their true vocation of reproducing 'A Healthy Race', into the pursuit of careers such as teaching.[32] As one observer stated, 'it is probably not an exaggeration to say, that to the average cost of each girl's education through high school must be added one unborn child'.[33] Home economics would theoretically lead future mothers – both college women and high school women – back to the nest by convincing them of the importance of their role as mothers.

Infant mortality was another social problem whose solution was linked to home economics. The seriousness of the problem is borne up in statistics: one fourth of all deaths in 1908 were children under five. While unsanitary milk storage, oppressive heat in tenements, general lack of attention to hygiene, and other problems associated with low wages and poverty were recognized as primary causal agents, it was believed that the root cause was the ignorance of mothers. As this was so eloquently stated by leaders of the AHEA: 'Our problem then is this; mothers untrained for motherhood on one side of the equation, and dead babies on the other side'.[34] One solution to the problem was to require girls and young women to be trained in mothercraft and the AASPIM (American Association for the Study and Prevention of Infant Mortality) was one of the organizations most active in the drive to reduce infant mortality rates through public school education. They proposed that girls and young women be required to study mothercraft.[35]

David Snedden, the Commissioner of Education for Massachusetts and a prominent vocational educator, spoke to this issue at the fifth annual meeting of the AASPIM. Following Snedden's talk on 'Some Possibilities of Public Schools in Reducing Infant Mortality', the committee on public school education submitted a resolution stating:

> Inasmuch as, ignorance of sanitation, personal hygiene and care of infants before and after birth is the commonest cause of infant mortality, and racial well-being requires conformity to laws of physical, mental, and social health that can be had universally only through specific education; Resolved: ... That for young adults and older: Instruction in Home Economics in all high schools, should include in courses for homemakers the care of infants and children.[36]

The health and welfare of industrial workers was yet another aspect of family life that home economics would ensure. Adelaide Hoodless, a prominent home economist in Canada, described the home as, 'the workshop for the making of men.'[37] Similarly Eva White, a well known home economist in the United States argued that, 'back of our industrial workers must be properly functioning homes ... our education system must meet the demands of home and industry'.[38] From the perspective of many people a socially and economically efficient system was one whereby 'food, refreshment, rest, the inspiration and strength which come from sympathy and affection, consolation and encouragement', are provided to workers by homemakers.[39]

In addition to keeping their spouses happy, women were advised to manage their pay checks efficiently and wisely. AHEA statistics cited in a congressional hearing on vocational education indicated that $1,000,000,000 could be saved every year if America's homemakers were educated properly.[40] We need to pay attention to the consumption of wealth advised Benjamin Andrews of Teachers' College, Columbia University; 'This means education for the "woman who spends" as well as the woman who produces'.[41] Consumer education included budgeting to stretch slim pay checks, buying the most nutritious foods and purchasing the expanding list of labor-saving devices available to the American home: vacuum cleaners, toasters, irons, and stoves.[42]

Domestic feminists who advocated education for future homemakers were supported by other progressive-era organizations and personalities, but there were significant distinctions between them. Family protection advocates such as sociologist Edward Ross argued for home economics based on a nineteenth century conception of woman's role. Their concern was that young women were deserting homemaking and childrearing responsibilities and that the social efficiency and stability of society were threatened by these dangerous trends. Women needed to be socialized back into their homemaking role and taught how to cook nutritious meals, keep attractive homes, and raise children properly.

The rationale for home economics offered by family protectionists such as Ross was based on the idea that women belonged at home doing traditionally defined housework and childrearing. Domestic feminists voiced the same concerns about the status of the family, and offered the same solution of home economics, but they were arguing from a feminist perspective which assumed women's superior ability in dealing with social reform problems and which necessitated the empowerment of women to deal with these problems. Home economics was the means by which the next generation of young women would be socialized into their role as municipal housekeepers and the means by which the science and technology needed to solve the complex community problems would be transferred. Moreover, home economics was the ticket to public life and a legitimate role in policy-making institutions. Domestic feminists, family protection advocates, and proponents of professional homemaking, such as Ellen Richards and Christine Frederick, shared a belief in the primacy of women's homemaking and mothering role. They all believed that women should maintain separate but equal spheres of influence and that home economics was the key to teaching the requisite special skills and to socializing young women for their roles. Beyond these significant areas of agreement, which provided a unity of purpose, it is clear that they differed in their vision of women's role. What seems most remarkable about these personalities and groups was that they were able to organize so successfully under one banner and ultimately influence the curricula of American schools.

Rural Home Advocates

Theodore Roosevelt's appointment of the Country Life Commission in 1908 signaled another significant progressive-era issue with implications for women's education, the rural life problem.[43] Whereas advocates of professional home-making hoped to stem the flow of women from home into the work place, supporters of rural home economics hoped to stem the flow of young women from farms into cities. Concern about diminishing rural populations and the demise of country living peaked in the first decade of the century. Although in 1910 as many as 54 per cent of the nation's families still lived in rural areas, the rural to urban demographic shift was well under way.[44] Many people were concerned about the 'exodus' of young people to cities. A contributor to *Vocational Education* wrote in 1914 that 'The constant cityward trend of population on the part of young people, who are born in the country, needs to be checked'.[45] The shifting demographics was mainly discussed in terms of young men because their absence affected farm productivity, however the exodus of young women was acknowledged as a problem as well. Using 1920 Census statistics the *New York Times* reported on the flight of farm women: 'Larger numbers of women than of men are leaving farms in search of more lucrative fields of endeavor'.[46] Farm women and men, educators, and legislators asked, how can we keep the girls on the farm? Schools and curricula were drawn into the general discussion with the criticism that school was 'unfitting our boys and girls for the work of their home communities'.[47] Rural life advocates proposed that curricula should be revised to meet the special needs of their students and that home economics in particular might help to keep girls on the farm.

Home economics was an important means to the preservation of country life according to its boosters. Relentless drudgery was a major complaint of life on a farm as a 1919 survey of farm life indicated; the average work day for women on the farm was 11.3 hours, and 87 per cent of women surveyed reported no vacation during the year.[48] Moreover, most women were hauling their own water from wells into their homes. Home economics curricula for young farm women included information about labor-saving appliances and methods to lighten the load of drudgery. Theoretically, home economics curricula would help lessen the gap between the quality of life for farm women and urban women.[49] Beyond stemming the flow of young women to the city, and improving the quality of life for farm women, supporters of home economics alleged that the quality of life for men on the farm would be improved as well. Girls and women needed to be educated about nutrition, health, and home nursing to ensure the welfare, and productivity of farm workers. Women were responsible for creating happy serene homes that would serve as models for the next generation of farm people, the children, and that would be places where farm men might like to 'linger'. The Secretary of Agriculture, a key promoter of home economics wrote:

> [woman is responsible for] Contributing the social and other features which make farm life satisfactory and pleasurable ... On her rests largely the moral and mental development of the children, and on her attitude depends ... the important question of whether the succeeding generation will continue to farm or will seek the allurements of life in the cities.[50]

A third objective was to enhance farm women's sense of partnership in the farm enterprise. Farm women's substantial contribution to the family economy was generally acknowledged and recent historical work by Joanne Vanek has validated this phenomenon: 'On the farm, husbands and wives were partners not only in making a home but also in making a living'.[51] Without women to run the farm house, raise the children, and administer the kitchen garden industries, farms were hard put to survive. The following characterization of farm families was a generally accepted view: 'My aunt, busy in and about the house was as strong a prop of the family's prosperity as my uncle afield with his team. Uncle knew it, and, what is more, she knew he knew it'.[52] Home economics programs were supposed to emphasize this aspect of the farm women's role and augment the training for the various cottage industries that farm women engaged in such as canning, poultry and butter making.[53] Smith Lever Agricultural Extension programs such as canning clubs organized in schools were heavily promoted for that reason.

It is significant that arguments for economic independence were conspicuously absent in the rhetoric of rural home economics despite the attempts of some women to broaden women's participation in farm life. Members of the Women's National Farm and Garden Association published articles about the need for women in farming, and agencies such as the NYCBVI (New York City Bureau of Vocational Information) developed success literature to sell the rewards of independent farming to women.[54] 'I certainly think that agriculture and stock raising is an open field for women. Any woman strong enough to do her own housework can do any and all the work on the farm ...', wrote one enthusiastic farmer to the NYCBVI.[55] Although much of this literature on the 'new profession' for women in rural settings was directed at women who could go on to an agricultural college and who would have access to capital, the argument for economic role expansion had profound implications for high school home economics and agricultural education. Yet the issue was not to be found in the rhetoric of rural life education.

The men and women who were involved in the 'Country Life Movement' were primarily concerned with preserving rural life and educating young people to appreciate the benefits of farm life and to assume their sex differentiated roles with pride; home economics was a major thrust of the movement. In contrast to domestic feminism, however, the rural home economics movement did not envision significant change in women's role. Improving the quality of women's lives so they would stay on the farm and rural life would be sustained was the main goal. As was true for the professional homemaking lobby, advocates hoped that home economics would sustain women's traditional role. Yet a traditional farm woman's role was substantially different from her city cousins. Farm women enjoyed a sense of status and equality by virtue of their economic contributions that were unparalleled in more urban settings, even though 'according to custom and law women were subordinate to men'.[56] Thus home economics paradoxically represented the maintenance of a traditional division of labor and the more contemporary goal of equality between the sexes.

'Lifting as We Climb'

Rationales for ensuring a domestic education for young black women resembled arguments for young white women but race added a significant dimension to the rhetoric. Black women's clubs were the cornerstone in progressive-era reform for blacks. They were organized and populated by middle class black women who believed that black women had a moral obligation to uplift the race and contribute to the general welfare. Education in a general sense and domestic science specifically, were seen as keys to racial uplift and self-help. Carol Perkins's historical research on the connections between liberal and vocational education for black women focuses on what she calls 'pragmatic idealism,' the linkages between education, racial progress and home economics. Lucy Laney typified black clubwomen in her belief that, '. . . race uplift could not be accomplished until "the burdens of ignorance of laws and rules of hygiene in the home" were lifted'.[57]

Nannie Helen Burroughs added another dimension to the rationale when she argued for the professionalization of domestic work. The founder of the National Training School for Women and Girls in Washington argued that vocational schools were the gateway to household engineering. 'If Negro women do not learn the art, they will surely lose out in another occupation . . .'[58] Thus, the 'cult of true womanhood' and the professionalizing of domestic work provided rationales for home economics in young black women's education – echoing familiar themes with particular meaning for young black women and whose job ceiling was clay rather than glass.

Conclusions

The paradox of home economics, that it encompassed both traditional and feminist values and ideas was the key to its appeal. Moreover, home economics offered remedies for many of the important social ills plaguing society at the time. 'The mission of the ideal woman is to make the whole world home like', and home economics was the means.[59] Men would be lured from saloons by good food cheerfully cooked in efficient kitchens; farm women would stay in the country and farm conditions would improve generally; middle class women's lives would take on new meaning through scientific homemaking and municipal housekeeping. Working class women would manage their husbands' pay checks better; immigrants would be Americanized; domestic service employees would perform more efficiently; race efficiency would improve; infant mortality would be reduced, and the quality of life for Americans in general would be substantially improved.

Beyond the explicit agenda of the movement – reform – was the underlying and compelling argument that home economics represented a vote for a woman's sphere that discouraged participation in the paid labor force except for domestic service. It was in that sense a strong prescription for traditional women's roles and one that was antithetical to the perspective of feminists such as Charlotte Perkins Gilman who predicated progress for women on economic independence. Moreover, some would argue that home economics represented a form of social control to direct young middle class women out of the labor market back into traditional homemaking roles, and to maintain the economic position of working women at the bottom of a segmented labor market. The home economics movement in general and the campaign to feminize curriculum in public school was based on manifest class biased assumptions. One of the most conspicuous strains in the rhetoric is the absence of working class women's voices. Yet the movement was far more than a design to maintain the economic status quo. Women were not simply victims of a system that was designed to rob them of economic independence: the shifting sands of social and economic roles, race, demography and class are far too complex for a simplistic casting. Men and women worked together and separately mediating their own particular agendas based on race, class and gender in promoting home economics in the schools. For many women, home economics and the proper socialization of young women represented an optimistic vision of women's potential – that of municipal house-keepers empowered to effect change in the world. For some it was a means to reclaim the skills and knowledge that were women's ancient heritage and exclusive domain.[60] For yet others, home economics represented the assurance of a future supply of well trained domestic labor and the sustenance of a life style. For farm women and men, it meant the preservation of rural living and values, while for black women, it represented improved life conditions. In short, the rhetoric and promise of home economics were as complex and as broad as the scope of gender, race, and class questions during the Progressive era.

Notes

1 Beecher, C. (1843) *Treatise on Domestic Economy for the Use of Young Ladies at Home and at School*, Boston, T.H. Webb & Co., in Sklar, K.K. (1973) *Catharine Beecher: A Study in American Domesticity*, New Haven, Yale University Press, p. 152.

2 Craig, H. (1945) *The History of Home Economics*, New York, Practical Home Economics, pp. 11–22, passim; Richards, E. (1903) 'The Present Status and Future Development of Domestic Science Courses in High School', in *Fourth Yearbook of the National Society for the Scientific Study of Education*, Bloomington, Pantagraph Printing and Stationery Company, pp. 39–52.

3 Allen, G. (1889) 'Plain Words on the Woman Question', *The Popular Science Monthly*, reprinted in Newman, M. (1985) (Ed.) *Men's Ideas/Women's Realities, Popular Science, 1870–1915*, New York, Pergamon Press, pp. 125–131; Calhoun, A.W. (1919) *The Social History of the American Family From the Colonial Times to the Present*, 3 Volumes, *Since the Civil War*, III Cleveland, Arthur C. Clarke, pp. 85–116.

4 Hamilton, A.J. (1906) 'What Kind of Education is Best Suited for Girls', NEA (National Education Association) *Addresses and Proceedings*; Arnold, S.L. (1908) 'The Reconcilement of Cross-Purposes in the Education of Women', NEA *Addresses and Proceedings*, pp. 93–99.

5 Arnold, S., Ibid., pp. 93–99.

6 Harkness, M.L. (1914) 'The Education of the Girl', *Atlantic Monthly*, 113, p. 325.

7 Lasch, C. (1977) *Haven in a Heartless World*, New York, Basic Books, pp. 1–13; Sanford, E. (1913) *The Unrest of Women*, New York, D. Appleton and Company, passim.

8 Rothman, S.M. (1978) *Woman's Proper Place, A History of Changing Ideals and Practices, 1870 to the Present*, New York, Basic Books, pp. 98–106.

9 Hickok, Mrs J. (1916) 'The Business of Homemaking', *The Journal of Home Economics*, 8, No. 8, p. 442.

10 Willard, E. (1919) 'An Address to the Public, Particularly to the Members of the Legislature of New York, proposing A Plan for Improving Female Education', Middlebury, Middlebury College, cited in Williamson, M. (1942) 'The Evolution of Homemaking Education, 1818–1919', unpublished Ph.D. dissertation, Stanford University, pp. 17–24.

11 Sklar, K.K. *Catharine Beecher: A Study in American Domesticity*, pp. 151–152.

12 Sklar, K. *Catharine Beecher: A Study in American Domesticity*, p. xiii.

13 Richards, E.S. (1909) 'Influence of Industrial Arts and Sciences Upon Rural and City Home Life: From the Standpoint of Domestic Science', NEA, *Addresses and Proceedings*, pp. 636–639; Rossiter, M. (1982) *Women Scientists in America, Struggles and Strategies to 1940*, Baltimore, Johns Hopkins University Press, pp. 68–70; Richards, E.S. (1903) 'The Present Status and Future Development of Domestic Science Courses in High School', *The Fourth Yearbook of the National Society for the Scientific Study of Education*, Bloomington, Pantagraph Printing and Stationery Company, 2, pp. 39–51.

14 Frederick, C. (1916) *The New Housekeeping, Efficiency Studies in Home Management*, New York, Doubleday, Page & Company, passim; Taylor, F.W. (1911, 1967) *The Principles of Scientific Management*, New York, Norton.

15 Frederick, C. (1915) *Household Engineering: Scientific Management in the Home*, Chicago, American School of Home Economics, p. 33.

16 Ibid., p. 233; Frederick, C. 'Home Making', Lecture 15 of the course, 'Women in Industry: Her Opportunities in Business Today', in the papers of the NYCBVI (New York City Bureau of Vocational Information), B-3, Box 1, Folder 18, pp. 1–30, Schlesinger Library, Radcliffe College.

17 Frederick, C. 'Home Making'.

18 Blake, K.D. (1916) 'Thrift in Relation to the Home', NEA, *Addresses and Proceedings*, p. 220.

19 See Latimer, J.F. (1958) *What's Happened to our High Schools?* Washington, DC, Public Affairs Press, p. 145; Rutherford, M. (1977) 'Feminism and the Secondary School Curriculum, 1890–1920', unpublished Ph.D. dissertation, Stanford University, p. 152.

20 Lemons distinguished between the 'hard core' feminists who believed that progress for women was dependent on women's rights and suffrage and 'social feminists' who believed that social reform would lead to the emancipation of women. Blair uses the term 'domestic feminists', and Jane Addams's contemporaries used the term 'Municipal Housekeepers'; Blair, K. (1980) *The Clubwoman as Feminist, True Womanhood Redefined, 1868–1914*, New York, Holmes and Meier Publishers, Inc., p. 4.; Harper, I.H. (1909) 'Woman's Broom in Municipal Housekeeping', *Federation Bulletin*, June, p. 246; Lemons, J.S. (1975) *The Woman Citizen, Social Feminism in the 1920's*, Urbana, University of Illinois Press, p. viii.

21 Addams, J. (1914) 'The Larger Aspects of the Woman's Movement', *The Annals of The American Academy of Political and Social Science*, 56 November, pp. 1–8.

22 Chadsey, M. (1915) 'Municipal Housekeeping', *The Journal of Home Economics*, 7, 2, pp. 53–59.

23 Gilman, C.P. *Women and Economics*, in Schneir, M. (1972) (Ed.) *Feminism, The Essential Historical Writings*, New York, Vintage Books, pp. 230–246.

24 Reynolds, M. (1916) 'The Woman of Today', *The Journal of Home Economics*, 8, 12, p. 191.

25 Norton, A.P. (1914) 'The Renovation of the Home Thru Home Economics', NEA *Addresses and Proceedings*, pp. 618–622.

26 O'Neill, W. (1967) *Divorce in the Progressive Era*, New Haven, University of Connecticut, p. 20.

27 Dorr, R.C. (1910) *What Eight Million Women Want*, Boston, Small, Maynard & Company, passim.

28 Weatherly, U.G. (1909) 'How Does the Access of Women to Industrial Occupations React on the Family', *Papers and Proceedings Third Annual Meeting American Sociological Society*, 3, pp. 128–129.

29 Weir, L.H. (1917) 'Housing and Homemaking', NSPIE (National Society for the Promotion of Industrial Education), *Bulletin 24*, p. 240.

30 Honorable Carroll S. Page, (R, VT) (1912) 'Vocational Education', speech de-

livered in the United States Senate, 62nd Congress, 2nd session, 5 June 1912, *Senate Document 845*, Washington, DC, GPO, p. 52.

31 Ross, E.A. commentary on Howard's paper 'Is Freer Granting of Divorce an Evil', American Sociological Society, *Papers and Proceedings Third Annual Meeting*, p. 177.

32 Carlton, F. (1906) 'Broad Aspects of Race Suicide', *Arena*, 36 December, pp. 607–612; Penrose, C.A. (MD) (1914) 'A Nation's Life Depends on Men's Fighting Efficiency', *New York Times*, 4, October, 1914.

33 Greene, Mrs C. (1915) 'Child Welfare Work', *Federation Bulletin*, April, pp. 26–28.

34 (1916) 'News from the Field', *The Journal of Home Economics*, January, p. 51.

35 Andrews, B. (1914) 'Education for the Home', USBE (United States Bureau of Education), *Bulletin 1914*, No. 36, Whole Number 610.

36 (1915) 'Infant Mortality Conference', *The Journal of Home Economics*, January, p. 50.

37 Hoodless, A. (1910) 'The Education of Girls', NSPIE *Bulletin No.10, Proceedings, Third Annual Meeting*, March, p. 179.

38 White, E. 'The Place of Homemaking in Industrial Education for Girls', NSPIE *Bulletin No. 18, Proceedings Seventh Annual Meeting*, Peoria, Manual Arts Press, p. 137.

39 Gillette, J. *Vocational Education*, New York, American Book Company, p. 111.

40 Honorable Carroll S. Page, 'Vocational Education', p. 53.

41 Andrews, B. 'Education for the Home', p. 20.

42 Strasser, S. (1982) *Never Done*, New York, Pantheon Books, pp. 76–84.

43 Cremin, L.A. (1964) *The Transformation of the School, Progressivism in American Education 1876–1957*, New York, Vintage Books, pp. 75–85.

44 Cremin, L., pp. 75–85.

45 Brown, H.A. (1914) 'The New Hampshire Type of Reconstructed High School', *Vocational Education*, May, p. 337.

46 (1922) 'More Women Leave Farm', *New York Times*, November, reprinted in Janeway, E. (1973) (Ed.), *Women Their Changing Roles*, New York, Arno Press, p. 127.

47 Holton, E. (1912) 'Public Schools and Community Life', *Vocational Education*, May, p. 351.

48 Vanek, J. (1980) 'Work, Leisure, and Family Roles: Farm Household in the United States, 1920–1955', *Journal of Family History*, 5, No. 4, Winter, p. 422.

49 Johnson, D.B. (1913) 'Education of Women in the Country', in *Education in the South, Bulletin No. 30*, USBE, pp. 41–45; (1916) 'The Rural Home and the Farm Woman', NEA *Addresses and Proceedings*, p. 36; McKeever, W.A. (1912) *Farm Boys and Farm Girls*, New York, Macmillan Company, p. 237.

50 Quoted in Bevier, I. (1917) 'The Development of Home Economics', *Journal of Home Economics*, 9, no. 1, January, p. 4.

51 Vanek, J. 'Work, Leisure, and Family Roles', p. 422.

52 Vanek, J. 'Work, Leisure, and Family Roles', p. 423.

53 (1916) 'The Girls' Canning Clubs', *The Journal of Home Economics*, June–July, p. 316.

54 Loines, H. (1920) 'Those Who Love the Soil', *Association Monthly*, a publication of the Women's National Farm and Garden Association, June, p. 288, in papers of the NYCBVI, Box 2, Folder 28, Schlesinger Library; Devenhom, A. (1916) 'Women on the Land', *Women's Employment*, 16 Jan, 21, p. 4; Geer, C.T. (1918) 'Out of the Kitchen into the Fields', *House Beautiful*, 44, September, pp. 184–185; (1914) *Vocations for the Trained Woman*, Boston, WEIU (Women's Educational and Industrial Union), pp. 122–167.

55 (1918) Letter from Mrs Theodore Saxon to Mrs Emma Hirth, 1 January, in papers of the NYCBVI, B-3, Box 2, Folder 31, Schlesinger Library.
56 Vanek, J. 'Work, Leisure and Family Roles', p. 243.
57 Perkins, C. (1987) 'Pragmatic Idealism: Industrial Training, Liberal Education and Women's Special Needs. Conflict and Continuity in the Experience of Mary McLeod Bethune and Other Black Educators', unpublished Ph.D. dissertation, Claremont College and San Diego State University. passim.
58 Giddings, P. (1985) *When and Where I Enter, the Impact of Black Women on Race and Sex in America*, New York, Bantam Books, p. 102.
59 Giddings, p. 102.
60 Ehrenreich, B. and English, D. (1979) *For Her Own Good: 150 Years of the Experts' Advice To Women*, New York, Anchor Press, pp. 149–157.

3   Trade Education for the Woman Who Toils

As a contributor to *Manual Training Magazine* observed in 1912, 'the problem of trade instruction for young women is a new one and a complicated one'.[1] Even though the content of trade education which was generally needlework was not new, the notion of an educational program that would train young women for industrial employment was both new and controversial in the Progressive Era. Florence Marshall, a prominent advocate of trade training for women and director of the Manhattan Trade School for Girls, astutely observed that, '... while industrial training for women insofar as it is applied to the obvious activities of the home is hailed with delight, any specific training to place girls in skilled trades has at present more enemies than friends'.[2]

The issue of trade education for young women emerged at a time when women's participation in the labor force was widely debated. Specific issues such as the effects of women's competition on men's wages and the effects of particular industries on women's physical and moral health were argued along with broader concerns about the role of women. The following chapter focuses on the debates over trade education for young women, the progressive-era attitudes toward women and work that gave rise to the debates, and the various perspectives adopted by organizations and individuals who were interested in the issue.

The 'Girl Question' in Trade Education

The key issue in the 'girl question' in trade training was, should young women be trained for industrial employment? and if so, what kind of employment? Many people, including vocational educators and administrators responsible for defining courses and programs, believed that 'Women ought not to be in factories and workshops; they ought to be in their homes'. Some argued that vocational trade training 'would lead to economic independence and ... economic independence would eventually destroy the home'.[3] Others alleged that vocational training was a bad investment because women were working primarily for pin money.[4] And yet others believed that work would 'unfit' women for marriage and motherhood.[5] These allegations and concerns reflected a pervasive progressive-era preoccupation with the changing roles of women and the effects of industrial employment on women and their families. Concerns about women

were drawn into discussions about vocational training generally and trade training specifically.

There was a concerned and influential network of people – mainly middle
class women – who worked to influence the course of trade training in the
schools. Representatives from women's organizations such as the NWTUL
(National Women's Trade Union League) and the WEIU (Women's Educational
and Industrial Union), social science researchers such as Elizabeth Butler and
Mary Van Kleeck, home economists such as Laura Drake Gill of Sewanee
College, and settlement house people such as Jane Addams, constituted the core
group of advocates. These supporters of industrial and trade training for young
women agreed on two major points; first, that indeed, schools should be responsible for providing training for women's future vocation(s); second, that
industrial and trade training were primarily directed toward working class children, especially those described as 'motor minded' or not bookish. 'Greater
industrial training is not usually the question with the middle class', wrote a
prominent social scientist in a lecture series about women and work.[6] Young
middle class women who could afford to stay in school would pursue teaching or
commercial work it was assumed, and working class women would drop out of
school before high school. Beyond these two given parameters, trade and industrial education was a muddy field that overlapped with home economics.

Trade, industrial and technical education were used interchangeably, sometimes referring to home economics work such as laundry and hand sewing, and
sometimes referring to training for wage work such as power sewing in a
clothing factory.[7] For example, the Lucy Flower Technical High School of
Chicago and the Girls' Technical High School of Cleveland emphasized in their
vision statements, the teaching of technical knowledge and scientific understanding such as was needed to 'establish and maintain' a well ordered home.[8] Plain
sewing, dressmaking and millinery were taught in both of these schools for the
benefit of young women who had to become 'self-supporting at an early age', yet
school administrators indicated that imparting technical skills for homemaking
was the primary emphasis. In contrast, the Worcester Trade School for Girls,
which opened in 1912 under the direction of Cleo Murtland, emphasized education for the trades, meaning gainful employment rather than home industries.
Teaching the trades was the explicit purpose of the school although supplemental
work would be provided in 'the usual academic instruction, physical education
... and cookery'.[9]

The central question that educators and advocates wrestled with was, should
schools train young women for presumably short term jobs in industry or for
their long term careers as homemakers? Moreover, if trade training were adopted
by public schools, should it be in feminine industries such as the needle trades
which would be useful for future homemakers, or should women 'claim all of
labor as their province?', as Olive Shreiner argued.[10] Some people argued from a
very traditional perspective that women's industry was homemaking and that
schools should train 'homemakers' not dieticians. These people tended to be
advocates of home economics as the only legitimate content for vocational
education courses, and domestic service as the only appropriate vocation for
young women who needed to work.[11] Others incorporated both traditional
assumptions and feminist perspectives, reasoning that women would have dual
roles – short time wage earner and long time homemaker – and that they should

be trained for both.[12] A third perspective reflected more feminism and less tradition; women should be trained for the job market through trade training comparable to that offered to young men. All three of these perspectives, which translated into concrete suggestions about trade and industrial training, represented prescriptions for progressive-era problems. The assumption that working women and girls needed to be protected from the oppression of workplace conditions was shared by almost all of the advocates of trade and industrial education. However the three main prescriptions that emerged indicated quite different visions of women's lives.

Concern for young working class women, as indicated, was a major precipitating factor in the development of trade education for young women. The Manhattan Trade School for Girls and the Boston Trade School for Girls followed the example set by the WEIU of Boston which opened classes in embroidery, dressmaking, crocheting, and millinery to 'make women more self supporting'.[13] The Boston Trade School for Girls opened with fourteen girls and two teachers in 1904; by 1919 the day enrollment for the school was reported to be 347 and extension enrollment 436.[14] The enrollment of the Manhattan Trade School for Girls grew from its original twenty students in 1902 to a reported enrollment of 1,495 in 1919.[15] The development and growth of these schools coincided with a period of intense interest in the effects of industrial employment on women and children.

Women and Paid Work

'Woman's invasion of the industrial world', was the way some people referred to women's expanded role in industry.[16] Newspapers and magazines such as the *New York Times*, and *Survey Magazine*, and more scholarly publications such as the *Annals of the American Academy of Political and Social Sciences* featured articles and research reports about the effects of long hours, low wages, and poor working conditions on the health of the female work force.[17] Ida Tarbell rather plaintively observed that nobody talks about the housekeeper. 'The only woman who interests us is the "woman in industry", that is, the woman who is earning her living in factories, shops and offices'.[18] Middle class women and men celebrated the fact that high school and college graduates could be architects, farmers, file clerks or teachers, or anything else they wanted to be. Yet they also lamented the presence of women in industrial occupations.[19] Young women who dropped out of school were the special objects of concern because their lack of education predicted their low position in the work force. Thirty-eight per cent of the female non-agricultural work force worked in manufacturing and mechanical industries or stores.[20]

> Something like 75 per cent of these young girls ... enter the most undesirable wage-earning occupations, those most inimical to health, and those often morally dangerous; those with a wage below the proper standard of living, most fluctuating and in every way least desirable for the condition of the worker,

wrote Anna Garlin Spencer in a 1908 vocational education publication.[21] It was the plight of these school leavers that concerned progressive reformers and educators who were the architects of trade education for women. Jane Addams and Margaret Dreier Robins were among the prominent progressive-era reformers representing settlement houses, women's clubs, labor organization activists, social science researchers and trade school directors who comprised the core group of advocates. They directed the nation's attention to the perceived and real problems of women workers and went on to propose solutions such as trade training for young women.

Documenting the conditions and life styles of young working women was an important strategy used by progressive reformers who lobbied for changes based on the results. Research reports such as Emilie Josephine Hutchinson's study of *Women's Wages*, Hazel Grant Orsmbee's work on *The Young Employed Girl*, and Susan Kingsbury and May Allinson's report, *A Trade School for Girls*, provided evidence of the need for vocational training.[22] Researchers such as Allinson and Kingsbury were alarmed at the drop out rate for young women; 60 per cent of the young women in Worcester in 1912 left school before reaching 15 years of age.[23] The number of girls under 16 who left school to take jobs was increasing, reported Allinson and Kingsbury, and they were taking unskilled jobs.[24] An investigation of 'working girls' attending the New York evening schools found that of the 4,511 young women who were employed and had dropped out of school before they reached high school, 41 per cent were working in manufacturing and mechanical purusits and 56 per cent were working in trade and transportation.[25] Young women in these industries were relegated to unskilled positions where they might check, inspect, label, paste, sort, wrap, pack, or fill, depending on the product involved.[26] According to Elizabeth Butler who conducted an investigation in Pittsburgh (1909) the vast majority of women who worked in the trades were in positions classified as not skilled that required little or no training.[27]

There were many elements of the factory system which researchers and investigators focused on. Low wages resulting from the piece system were a particular concern of the middle class reformers who investigated the factory system. The piece system was used as a basis for wages in unskilled jobs which meant that wages were determined by the quantity of goods processed, basted, sewed, counted, etc. This method of linking productivity and wages grew out of the clothing industry where women were paid for each piece of goods they made. For example, Elizabeth Butler found in her research on Pittsburgh, that one young woman spent her entire day folding the ends of boxes for crackers and putting a red stamp on the end. She was paid one cent per dozen and if she could make a hundred dozen a day, she would get a ten cent bonus, altogether $1.10. This amounted to $5.50 per week if she made her quota.[28] The median wage for young women in factory industries was $6.25 in 1913, and this was not a living wage according to critics of the factory system.

A high rate of turnover among young female workers was another result of the factory system that reformers deplored and frequently commented on. A WEIU investigation of industrial opportunities in some Massachusetts cities found that in one jewelry factory in Sommerville, Massachusetts, '5 out of every 6 workers leave in a year; another says the whole force shifts every year'.[30] Similarly, a New York state factory investigating commission found that in the confectionary industry in New York City, 45 per cent of the workers stayed four weeks or less.[31] An investigator of conditions in Worcester, Massachusetts reported that the unskilled beginning worker, 'drifts from place to place and never becomes proficient in any one thing'.[32]

The health of young women was another expressed concern of progressive reformers, feminists and social science researchers. Long hours of standing and doing repetitive work was believed to cause damage to women's reproductive systems and to cause birth defects when women did conceive. The cotton mills specifically, and poorly ventilated industrial concerns generally, were responsible for high rates of lung disease among young female workers. The mortality rate for women who worked exceeded that of all men by one-third.[33]

The moral health of women, especially young women, was an equally potent issue. While some people argued that women worked only for 'pin money' citing the interest of young women in buying clothes and finery as their evidence, social science researchers documented the number of women who worked to support their families on pitifully low wages. Prostitution and stealing were blamed on the low wages paid to young women who needed a living wage to support themselves and their dependants. As one progressive-era writer expressed it, 'There is always the hideous haven of prostitution menacing girls who are underpaid'.[34]

While historians have appropriately raised questions about the motivations of middle class reformers and their intense interest in working class lives, the historical record persuasively argues that workplace conditions were not particularly healthful, wages were low, and industry was generally hostile to the advancement of young women.[35] Investigations into the problems of young working class women documented the realities of their lives and provided reformers with evidence that supported intervention. Trade education advocates used the findings to argue for trade training. Progressive-era protectionism, coupled with the reality of workplace conditions, provided the context for discussion about vocational trade training. Although most interested parties agreed that working conditions for young women in industry posed serious problems, they did not agree on the solutions.

Perspectives

Protecting and educating 'working class daughters' was an explicit goal of the middle class reformers and feminists who lobbied for and informed the trade education movement. However trade education advocates held very different ideas on what protection and education meant.

One interpretation was that trade education should consist of training for housework. A small but vocal minority of women who represented the AHEA (American Home Economics Association), the GFWC (General Federation of Women's Clubs) and the WEIU argued for trade training that was exclusively in the 'home industries'. Such a scheme, from their perspective, would have solved a number of problems; low wages, unhealthful working conditions, the unsupervised lives that 'factory girls' allegedly lead, while providing training and modeling for their future homes.[36] Moreover, the 'servant problem,' that was often lamented in periodicals of the day, would be helped. The servant problem referred to the fact that household service was considered an undersirable occupation by most young women, and the number of available household servants was diminishing. 'Every day the demand for experienced household help grows', wrote a club woman in 1914.[37] The percentage of household workers relative to the total of female wage earners steadily dropped during the Progressive Era from 35.8 per cent in 1890 to 16.2 per cent in 1920.[38] The Boston YWCA conducted a widely quoted study of domestic service which validated what many suspected and feared. Young working women preferred factory and sales work to household employment which they found uninteresting, degrading, and confining.[39]

Proposals to limit definitions of trade training to domestic service amounted to arguments for a nineteenth century view of women, protected and excluded from the marketplace. Working class daughters needed maternal supervision because the factories and the workplace would surely take advantage of them, it was assumed. As one GFWC member put it, 'The women, innocent, unguarded, untrained, unprepared, are entering this [industrial] world ... Have you not, the mothers of the race, this great responsibility on your shoulders'.[40] Guidance and supervision were best provided, the advocates argued, in individual homes, where the 'work of the privileged educated woman for her little sisters', can influence the young woman's life and the life of her future family.[41] The school was to be a working partner in this process, providing an education that would fit this young woman for her appointed station in life, and at the same time improving the homes she came in contact with, those of middle class families.

The proposal to use public education funds for training working class girls for service did not go unnoticed. It was severely criticized as was a similar scheme proposed in Great Britain.[42] Moreover, as national policy, the idea was not popular. Florence Marshall, speaking for the NSPIE (National Society for the Promotion of Industrial Education) observed that while domestic and personal service deserved attention, they were not at present systematized or business like in their conduct, standards, and training, and that they had a long way to go before they could be classified as a trade.[43]

None the less, there were attempts to educate particular populations of young women for domestic service, and this was often done on the basis of class, race and ethnicity.

A second and more progressive perspective on trade training was advocated by the network of women who belonged to the NSPIE. The Sub-committee on Industrial Education for Women included such notable women as Jane Addams of Hull House, Mary Morton Kehew, Mary Schenck Woolman and Susan Kingsbury of the WEIU in Boston, Sophonisba Breckinridge of the University of Chicago's Department of Household Administration, and Florence Marshall who served on the Massachusetts Commission on Industrial and Technical Education and then became director of the Boston Trade School for Girls.[44] These women envisioned a trade education system for young women that would provide good pay, room for advancement, an understanding of the industrial system, and a skill that would serve them well in their eventual role as home-makers. In her role as secretary to the Sub-committee, Marshall outlined its position on industrial training for young women in a bulletin devoted to the topic. She wrote that the young woman should be taught skills that would lead to jobs in the needle trades and food industries and would provide the kind of skill, 'which she can best use in her home later'.[45] The women who supported the idea of dual roles argued that women must work. As Mary Shenck Woolman stated it:

> It is not a time for us to stand aside and say women should remain at home, even if that is an ideal ... Let us think for a moment of the situation of working girls in a busy industrial city. They must work for self-support. They must do it immediately. They should have a decent wage. They should have good health.[46]

In addition to asserting young women's right to training, however, they were also saying that it was appropriate that they be trained for marriage, or, at least, that the the work skills they were trained in be applicable to homemaking.

Susan · Kingsbury was a particularly influential member of the Sub-committee, involved in both research and activism. Kingsbury earned her master's degree in history from Stanford University and then migrated east to pursue a doctorate in colonial history at Columbia University.[47] She became interested in social research and worked on the investigation of early school leavers for the Massachusetts Commission on Industrial and Technical Education. This work introduced her to the problems of young women, and she then went to work for Mary Morton Kehew and the Boston WEIU doing research on young working women and assisting in the establishment of trade classes. Her most widely publicized work in this area was the study published by the USBE (United States Bureau of Education) entitled *A Trade School For Girls, A Preliminary Investigation in a Typical Manufacturing City, Worcester, Mass.*[48] In this study, Kingsbury and her colleague, May Allinson, surveyed the positions open to young women in skilled, semi-skilled and unskilled work. They made recommendations for training in the Worcester Trade School for Girls which focused on training in the feminine industries: power sewing machine operating, dressmaking, and millinery. Kingsbury exemplified the perspective of her colleagues on the NSPIE Sub-committee. She was genuinely concerned about young working women and believed that effective trade training should be offered in public schools. The proposed solution, training for 'feminine industries' represented a compromise of traditional values and feminism. Unlike the women who opposed women's presence in factories and lobbied for domestic service as trade training, the NSPIE recognized that young women were obviously going to work in factories and moreover, deserved training. Some argued that work was a desirable experience for young women because it gave them a sense of independence and self esteem. Most concurred that in the long run, young women would marry and thus they should work in feminine industries, both for the practice industries offered and the protected environments they provided. While these women defended women's right to work, they never challenged the conspicuous sex stereotyping that confined women to low paying jobs.

In contrast to the former two perspectives, the third was the least traditional and the most feminist. The NWTUL was foremost in promoting a concept of training that expanded and challenged accepted definitions of women's employment. In a 1913 position statement on the subject of vocational education the NWTUL called for total equity in vocational training with boys and girls studying the same subjects in co-educational schools.[49] NWTUL leaders, Margaret

Dreier Robins, Leonora O'Reilley, Alice Henry and Agnes Nestor were among the women convinced that economic equity, which translated into better jobs, was the key to uplifting the status of women.[50] They supported the more traditional feminists in their concern for family life, infant mortality, the health of mothers and future mothers, and the need to protect working women's interests. However, their solution was to educate female workers so they would have skills, wages and job ladders that were competitive with those available to young men. The women of the NWTUL shared this position with other individual women who were concerned about equity in the workplace. Emilie Josephine Hutchinson, a lecturer in economics at Barnard College wrote:

> If vocational education is merely imposed upon the present distribution of industry between men and women it will fall far short ... if vocational education attains to the measure of its possibilities for women it must be based on a sound analysis of the positions for which training is needed and a generous extension of this training to girls and women on equal terms with boys and men.[51]

The researcher and author of *Women in the Trades*, Elizabeth Butler, concluded that trade training based on cooperation between trade school and manufacturers was the key to improving the economic status of women. She asserted that by trade training she did not mean, 'The sort of training often most in demand, class work in amateur cooking, dressmaking, and millinery' – feminized work – instead, she meant 'class work comparable to that of trade-trained men'. She elaborated on this idea as follows:

> To be concrete; Pittsburgh women are largely employed in printing and bookbinding establishments, but as feeders, not as rulers. Why not teach them to mix inks, to fill pens, to manage the ruling machines ... Women are employed in machine shops and foundries. Why are they not taught the principles on which sand cores are made, the combinations of sand, the kinds of sands for different sorts of work.[52]

Thus Butler, Hutchinson and the NWTUL women were calling for a radically expanded definition of trade training for young women and ultimately sex equity and integration in the work place. This third vision of women's role was predicated on the knowledge that many working class women would be working for a good portion of their lives, and on the belief that economic independence was ultimately beneficial. Unlike the first two views on trade education, this perspective offered a strong argument for sex-integrated vocational training.

These three views of trade education represented different perspectives on the role of young women in the job market, and the differences clearly reflected society's persistent ambivalence about women in the work force generally and their presence in industry specifically. Some women and men argued from a very traditional perspective that women did not belong in the work force at all, while others asserted that women had always been there; they had merely followed their work out into industry and now they wanted '... labour and the training that fits us for labour!' As Ann Firor Scott pointed out however, traditional values and feminist values are not mutually exclusive, especially during a period of change. Thus the women who took the most feminist position on the role of women in the work force also argued that most women would be mothers and homemakers and that we needed to establish a 'living wage to guard the home'.[53]

The most popular position was a compromise that allowed for women's presence in the work force while it provided a protective influence over the kind of workplace. Mary Schenck Woolman's Manhattan Trade School for Girls was typical. It provided trade training in trades that were specified as feminine and mainly involved traditional needle trades. The succession of school directors and their colleagues in the women's trade education network argued for higher pay, access to other jobs in the system such as cutting and generally better working conditions, but they never seriously addressed the confinement of women's work to needle trades.

Their adherence to a narrow definition of trade training for women probably reflected their own deep ambivalence about women in industrial work. Despite the minority voice of women such as Leonora O'Reilley, who was raised in a working class, union supporting family, the ideal for most of the women in the trade education circle was middle class: women work for a few short years before marriage. Work after marriage was only out of necessity and would reflect badly on the husband's ability to care for his wife and family. Ultimately women's true profession was that of homemaker and mother. For Woolman, in the best of all circumstances, trade education and trade experience should provide preparation for that experience, and at the very least should not detract from that true profession.

Industrial employment of women was believed to cause a host of ills that the trade education lobby could not ignore. Their role, as they saw it was defensive; it was to educate for the eventuality of marriage while protecting women from the possible ill effects of industry. Thus the overriding influence on trade education perspectives was social ideology. If, as Sarah Eisenstein observed in *Give Us Bread But Give Us Roses*, young blue collar workers saw work as a temporary way station on the road to marriage, and if 'the tendency to see marriage as an escape from the shop or factory was engendered by the condition under which women worked' there was little in trade education rhetoric to challenge this view of work.[54]

Notes

1   Hildreth, H. (1912) 'Vocational Training for Girls and Women', *Vocational Education*, 1, p. 366.
2   Marshall, F. (1909) 'The Industrial Training of Women', *The Annals of the American Academy of Political and Social Science*, 33, January–June, p. 120.
3   Fletcher, F. (1915) 'Vocational Education and Guidance', *General Federation of Women's Clubs Magazine*, March, p. 35.
4   The 'pin money' argument produced a flood of studies to prove that women were insufficiently paid and frequently self-supporting. See WEIU (Women's Educational and Industrial Union) Research Department, (1911) *The Living Wage of Women Workers*, New York, Longmans, Green and Company; (1974) *Working Girls of Cincinnati*, New York, Arno Press; Kelley, F. (1916) 'Minimum Wage Legislation', *American Labor Yearbook*, New York, Rand School of Social Sciences, p. 61.

5   Weatherly, U.G. (1907) 'How Does the Access of Women to Industrial Occupa-
    tions React Upon the Family', *The Annals of the American Academy of Political and
    Social Science*, 27, March, pp. 124–133.
6   Poyntz, J.S. 'Woman as An Economic Factor – a History of the Woman Move-
    ment', Lecture 2, Women in Industry Lecture Series in the papers of the
    NYCBVI (New York City Bureau of Vocational Information), Box 1, Folder 6,
    Schlesinger Library, Radcliffe College.
7   'Blue Collar' is not an expression that was generally used to describe women's
    jobs in industry during the Progressive Era, however since then it has come into
    general use. It mainly refers to industrial occupations, especially those requiring
    unskilled, semi-skilled and skilled labor. Domestic service is not generally de-
    scribed as blue collar work even though it may be comparable to housekeeping
    work in industry. Occupations that are now referred to as pink collar – clerical
    work and beauticians work – did not fall under the general rubric of blue collar
    work as well, even though they may have been similar in some respects. For a
    discussion of sex-typing in blue collar work see Matthaei, J.A. (1982) *An Econo-
    mic History of Women in America*, New York, Schocken Books, pp. 209–218.
8   (1911) 'Vocational Training in Chicago', *Vocational Education*, May, 52; (1907)
    'The Technical High School', The GFWC (General Federation of Women's
    Clubs) *The General Federation Bulletin*, June, p. 328; (1912) 'A New Chicago
    School for Girls', *Vocational Education*, May, p. 369.
9   Ibid., p. 369.
10 Schreiner, O. (1975) *Woman and Labour*, Johannesburg, Cosmos Publications
    Ltd., reprint of 1911 edition New York, Fred A. Stokes.
11 Hoodless, A. 'The Education of Girls,' NSPIE (National Society for the Pro-
    motion of Industrial Education), *Bulletin No.10, Proceedings, Third Annual Meet-
    ing*, p. 179.
12 Marshall, F. 'Industrial Training for Women,' NSPIE *Bulletin Number 4*, 1907,
    p. 7.
13 Donham, A. 'History of the Women's Educational and Industrial Union', in
    Papers of the WEIU of Boston, B-8, Unprocessed Collection, Carton 1, Folder
    11.
14 See 'History of the Boston Trade School for Girls', in papers of the NYCBVI,
    Box 7, Folder 55, Schlesinger Library, Radcliffe College.
15 Goodsell, W. (1924) *The Education of Women, Its Social Background and Its Prob-
    lems*, New York, MacMillan Company, p. 179.
16 (1912) *Manual Training Magazine*, May, p. 366.
17 (1913) 'Tuberculosis' Harvest Among Women in the Cotton Mills', *New York
    Times*, 29 June, reprinted in Janeway, *Women: Their Changing Roles*, pp. 50–53;
    (1919) 'The Third Sex in Industry', *New York Times*, 30, March, reprinted in
    Janeway, pp. 69–70; (1903) 'The Employment of Women', *Popular Science Month-
    ly*, 73, October, pp. 571–572; Keir, Dr M. (1913) 'Women in Industry', *Popular
    Science Monthly*, 83, October, pp. 375–380; Stokes, R.P. (1906) 'The Condition
    of Working Women from the Working Woman's Viewpoint', *The Annals of the
    American Academy of Political and Social Science*, 27, No. 3 May, pp. 165–175;
    Weatherly, U.G. (1907) 'How Does the Access of Women to Industrial Occupa-
    tions React Upon the Family', *The Annals of the American Academy of Political and
    Social Science*, 27, March, pp. 124–133; Yudelson, S. (1904) 'Woman's Place in
    Industry and Labor Organizations', *Annals of the American Academy of Political and
    Social Science*, 24, No. 2, September, pp. 343–350.
18 Tarbell, I. (1913) 'What Industrial Training Should We Give the Average Girl?'
    Bulletin No. 18, Proceedings of Fifth Annual Meeting, p. 132.
19 Kennedy, S.E. (1979) 'Poverty, Respectability, and Ability to Work', *Internation-
    al Journal of Women's Studies*, 2, No. 5, September/October, p. 401.

20 Ormsbee, H.G. (1927) *The Young Employed Girl*, New York, The Woman's Press, passim; Rotella, E.J. (1981) *From Home to Office, US Women at Work 1870–1930*, Ann Arbor, UMI Research Press, p. 25.

21 Spencer, A.G. 'The Social Value of Industrial Education for Girls', NSPIE *Bulletin No. 6, Proceedings of the First Annual Meeting, Chicago*, p. 39.

22 Allinson, M. and Kingsbury, S. (1913) 'A Trade School for Girls, A Preliminary Investigation in a Typical Manufacturing City, Worcester, Mass', USBE (United States Bureau of Education) *Bulletin 1913*, No. 17, p. 13; Ormsbee, H.G. *The Young Employed Girl*; Hutchinson, E.J. (1919) *Women's Wages, A Study of the Wages of Industrial Women and Measures Suggested to Increase Them*, Doctoral dissertation, Columbia University.

23 Allinson, M. and Kingsbury, S. 'A Trade School for Girls', p. 13.

24 Allinson, M. and Kingsbury, S. 'A Trade School for Girls', p. 14.

25 Gruenberg, B.C. (1916) 'Compulsory Education Laws', *American Labor Year Book*, p. 306; Van Kleeck, M. *Working Girls in Evening Schools*, New York, Survey Associates Inc., p. 94.

26 (1916) *American Labor Yearbook*, p. 267; Burdick, A. (1919) 'The Wage-Earning Girl and Home Economics', FBVE (Federal Board for Vocational Education) *Vocational Summary*, 2, No. 1, May, p. 56; Douglas, P. (1921) *American Apprenticeship and Industrial Education*, New York, Longmans, Green & Company, Agents, pp. 132–175.

27 Butler, E. (1909) *Women and the Trades, Pittsburgh 1907–1908*, New York, Russell Sage, p. 369; Odencrantz, L. (1919 reprint 1977) *Italian Women in Industry*, New York, Arno Press, p. 43.

28 Butler, E. *Women and the Trades*, p. 65.

29 Shientag, B. 'An Argument in Support of Minimum Wage Legislation for Women and Minors in Industry in the State of New York', from the papers of the NYCBVI, Box 5, Folder 75, Schlesinger Library, Radcliffe College.

30 Allinson, M. and Kingsbury, S. (1913) 'A Trade School for Girls, A Preliminary Investigation in a Typical Manufacturing City, Worcester, Mass.', USBE *Bulletin 1913*, No. 17, p. 13.

31 Osgood, I. 'Labor Legislation, Minimum Wage, Working Men's Compensation,' Lecture 13, NYCBVI papers, Box 1, Folder 16.

32 Allinson, M. and Kingsbury, S. (1913) 'A Trade School for Girls', p. 12.

33 'Tuberculosis' Harvest Among Women in the Cotton Mills', *New York Times*, 29 June; Stokes, R.H.P. 'The Condition of Working Women From the Working Woman's Viewpoint', p. 629; Harris, A.K. (1982) *Out to Work, A History of Wage-Earning Women in the United States*, New York, Oxford University Press, p. 107.

34 Nearing, S. (1916) 'Low Wages and Prostitution', *The American Labor Yearbook, 1916*, p. 282; (1913) 'Low Wages and Vice, Are They Related?' *Life and Labor*, May, p. 108.

35 MacLean, A. (1916) *Women Workers and Society*, Chicago, A.C. McLurg, p. 8.

36 'School of Housekeeping,' brochure of the Boston WEIU 'Course for Employees', Papers of the WEIU, Box 1, Folder 5, Schlesinger Library, Radcliffe College.

37 Andrews, B.R. (1915) 'Education for the Home', USBE *Bulletin 1914*, No. 36, Pt.2, Washington, DC, GPO.

38 Fitzgerald, H. (1914) 'Domestic Science or Home-Making', *General Federation of Women's Clubs's Magazine*, 12, June, p. 49.

39 Katzman, D. (1978) *Seven Days A Week, Women and Domestic Service in Industrializing America*, Chicago, University of Illinois Press, p. 52.

40 (1912) *The Federation Bulletin*, September, p. 460.

41 (1911) *The Federation Bulletin*, July, p. 540.

42 (1915) 'Housekeeper's Department', *The Journal of Home Economics*, December, p. 549; Dyehouse, C. (1977) 'Good Wives and Little Mothers: Social Anxieties and the Schoolgirl's Curriculum, 1890–1920', *Oxford Review of Education*, 3, No. 1, pp. 21–22.

43 Marshall, F. (1911) 'Part 1, Trade Education for Girls', NSPIE *Bulletin No. 13, Proceedings Fourth Annual Convention, Boston, Massachusetts*, January, p. 19.

44 Ibid.

45 Marshall, F. 'Part I, Trade Education for Girls', NSPIE *Bulletin No. 13*, p. 13.

46 Woolman, M.S. (1911) 'New Requirements Made by the Trade Schools', NSPIE *Bulletin No. 13, Proceedings, Fourth Annual Meeting, Boston, Massachusetts*, January.

47 For information on Susan Myra Kingsbury see James, E.T. *et al.* (Eds) *Notable American Women*, 2, p. 335.

48 Allison and Kingsbury, 'A Trade School for Girls'.

49 (1913) 'Fourth Biennial Outlines Educational Work', *Life and Labor*, August, p. 236, in microfilm edition, 'Papers of the Women's Trade Union League and Its Principal Leaders', Schlesinger Library, Radcliffe College.

50 Henry, A. (1973) 'Women and Vocational Training,' *The Trade Union Woman*, New York, Burt Franklin, pp. 195–216; Miller, R.J. 'Introduction, Papers of the Women's Trade Union League and Its Principal Leaders', pp. 19–26.

51 Hutchinson, J. *Women's Wages*, p. 172; Mary Anderson of the Women's Bureau, Department of Labor, was also supportive of equity in vocational training, see (1921) 'Vocational Guidance', in papers of the NYCBVI, B-3, Box 17, Folders 226–228.

52 Butler, E. *Women and the Trades*, p. 374.

53 Schreiner, O. *Woman and Labour*, p. 132.

54 'A living wage for mothers who must earn', was adopted by the NWTUL (National Women's Trade Union League) as a slogan and appeared on a graphic depicting a mother at a sewing machine with a baby in arms. See 'Papers of the Women's Trade Union League and Its Principal Leaders', microfilm edition.

4   Commercial Education for
the Office 'Girl'

In this discussion of prescriptions and vocational education curricula, commercial education stands out as an anomaly: it was as conspicuous in its absence from discussion as it was remarkable in its growth. Vocational educators and women's organizations did not lobby for or against commercial education. The NSPVE (National Society for the Promotion of Vocational Education), the organizational voice for vocational training issues, published very little on the topic in its bulletins and did not feature the topic in its annual presentations.

Why did it generate so little interest among the vocational educators and interest groups anxious to debate the comparative merits of trade education or home economics for women? There were two related reasons. One is that it was considered to be a middle class vocation much like teaching. Vocational education lobbies focused on the interests of working class students who either would not attend high school or would limit their tenure there. As Kantor explains it, 'in fact middle class career interests were not well respected in the vocational education lobbies'. Commercial education was a field for students who could go to high school and who could consider a middle class occupation. The other related reason is that commercial education was not linked to broad social concerns as were home economics and trade education. There was no reason to be concerned about the health and virtue of office workers because offices had become respectable places to work. In fact they were considered by some to be good training grounds for marriage. This image of middle class respectability evolved with the development of commercial education. Thus, like teaching which was an occupation that young women aspired to, there were no vocal advocates.

Commercial education emerged as an important field of study during the latter years of the nineteenth century. Private schools and commercial colleges expanded in response to a growing demand for office workers, and enrollment grew from 6,460 in 1871 to 91,549 in 1900.[1] This demand was the product of economic growth: the advent of large scale production where 'the mills grew larger ... and the work processes more minutely subdivided and dependent on machinery'. Moreover, there was the expanding presence of department stores such as Sears Roebuck and Montgomery Wards.[2] With its new mode of work the workplace required an army of clerical workers to monitor the changed production system. Private schools and eventually public schools adapted their curriculum to meet workplace needs.[3]

Women were increasingly welcomed into office work as the nineteenth century came to a close. The number of women office workers rose from less than 1,000 in 1870 to 100,000 by 1910 and to 1,000,000 by 1920.[4] These women were employed as stenographers and typists, bookkeepers, cashiers and accountants, clerks and private secretaries. They were well paid by the standards of the day; $11.00 was the average wage for office workers in Boston in 1912 as compared to the $8.00 earned by three-fifths of store employees.[5] Moreover, with additional skills learned in night school, for example, young women could advance up the ladder of positions, and theoretically increase their social contacts for husband searching, but there were critics of women's working presence in offices, especially in the late nineteenth century, just as there was criticism of all public domains 'invaded' by women. Office women were characterized as silly incompetents, as in the *Harper's Bazaar* engraving that showed women 'preening themselves before a mirror, fixing each other's hair, reading *Harper's Bazaar*, spilling ink on the floor'.[6] Their morality was questioned, as well as their physical stamina.

As the need for inexpensive docile, office workers grew, however, women were more often viewed as uplifting influences for the former male bastions and offices were soon thought of as good places for women to work. The man who wrote in the *New York Times* that, 'skirts and trousers side by side accomplish little work and many blunders', was honored with a reply from office worker Mary Smith who stated the new and enlightened view of office work.[7] 'The girls in the offices do not expose their qualities to contamination, but rather make an office better for their being there'.[8] Mary Smith argued, as did many of her contemporaries that office work was good training for marriage, and that 'If every woman in the United States had a year or more in a downtown office that woman would make some a better wife because of her wider understanding'.[9]

By 1913, offices were thoroughly redeemed as centers of female employment. Social workers interviewed for a survey on office work extolled its virtues as follows:

> The office secures the advantages of a refined environment; the work itself has cultural value, awakens responsibility, develops character, and promotes standards of achievement; hours are easy; pay is more generous than in the case of the store and the factory: incentive to advance is quite general; and social standing is better than in any other available form of work open to girls.[10]

Schools played an important role in facilitating women's presence in offices. Janice Weiss argued in her thesis on commercial education in the US that public educators incorporated commercial education into their high schools in order to expand high school enrollments.[11] The number of public high school students enrolled in business education jumped from 68,890 in 1900 to 430,975 in 1924, and the percentage of female students enrolled in commercial education courses jumped from 57 in 1914 to 66 in 1924.[12] The superintendent of the Boston Public Schools included a comment on the drawing power of commercial courses in his 1911 Report stating: 'it looked as though that line of work would be so crowded as to be disastrous'.[13] Occupational surveys such as Joseph Denburg's and the United States Office of Education's 1916 survey of San Francisco confirmed the popularity of the commercial course; office work was second only to teaching as the preference for most young women.[14]

In spite of a receptive labor market and accommodating schools however, there was very little support for commercial education within the vocational training movement. Almost nothing was written about the subject by vocational educators. The reasons for the boycott by the women's vocational training network had to do with the characteristics of commercial work, and the young women who were drawn to it, as well as the progressive-era agenda of the women who supported vocational training. In a lecture series on women and careers held in 1915, one woman noted that 'there is a distinctly social sense that the girl who is in an office is a little better than the girl who is selling'.[15] Similarly David Snedden, the editor of *Vocational Education Magazine* wrote that 'commercial education is more profitable and respectable than the pursuits of farmer and trade workers, to say nothing of the domestic servants and factory operatives'.[16] This image of respectability and status clung to commercial education and set it apart from blue collar occupations. Commercial education was a middle class white collar occupation that required some literacy, had a ladder of advancement through various skills and a position at the top, the private secretary. It was closest in status and training to teaching, which required high school training, and was in fact an alternative that had the additional advantage of requiring less training, (depending on the kind of job pursued), and fewer life style restrictions.

Because commercial education was distinct in both the level of training and status, it was not considered an occupation for grammar school or junior high school dropouts, nor was it originally thought of as a 'working class' job. In fact, in London, where the feminization of clerical work happened at the same time as in the United States, 'Women office workers tended to come from a different [higher] social class than the men who did the same work and the low pay and, consequently low standard of living, were an embarrassment to them [the women]'.[17]

The fact that office work had the image of being a middle class occupation for young women who could afford to stay in school meant that the progressive-era reformers who were the backbone of the women's vocational training movement were not interested in it. They did not see it as a subject that fell within their purview any more than teaching did, which was also clearly a vocation for which secondary schools trained. Such women as Jane Addams, Mary Schenck Woolman, and Susan Kingsbury became involved in vocational education because they wanted to see young women provided with a means of making a living. They focused their attention on early school leavers and working class women and made numerous assumptions about what was appropriate, desirable and feasible, concentrating mainly on feminine industries. For the individual women and the organizations who shaped the issues, the connections between the progressive-era agenda of protection – protecting health, virtue and the future of family life – and commercial education were non-existent.

The vocational training lobby had a fairly explicit agenda. They were women concerned about the welfare of working class women and the maintenance of separate spheres. Commercial education did not fit their interests or their definition of vocational education. The only persons who might have raised the issue were lobbyists for equal access in trade training such as the NWTUL (National Women's Trade Union League). They however, were very critical of 'pretentious office workers', and throughout the history of the league showed only the slightest interest in office work.[18] They were mainly interested in legitimizing blue collar work and protecting women workers, and were not inclined to support any issue or program that fostered what they perceived to be class hierarchies.

The case of commercial education illustrates very clearly the difficulties associated with applying an argument of economic control. The dominant factor in commercial education was gender related. While it especially appealed to middle class parents or those who could afford education, it attracted students from the working class and middle class much like teaching did. In Canada as well as the United States, commercial education did not attract reform interest. Without the support of women's organizations who were primarily responsible for ensuring a place for women in the vocational education movement generally, or vocational educators, there was little chance that commercial education would be included as vocational education. In fact it was not until 1963 that business education was included under the rubric of vocational education and thereby provided with federal funding.

Notes

1 WEIU (Women's Educational and Industrial Union,) (1914) *The Public Schools and Women in Office Service*, Boston, pp. 4–9; Weiss, J. (1978) 'Education for Clerical Work: A History of Commercial Education in the US since 1850', Ed. D. dissertation, Harvard University, pp. 16–73.

2 Rogers, D.T. (1978) *The Work Ethic in Industrial America, 1850–1920*, Chicago, University of Chicago, pp. 23, 27.

3 Davies, M.W. (1982) *Woman's Place Is at the Typewriter, Office Work and Office Workers, 1870–1930*, Philadelphia, Temple University Press, p. 250.

4 Hooks, J.M. (1947) 'Women's Occupations Through Seven Decades', Women's Bureau Bulletin No. 218 Washington, DC, GPO, pp. 75, 102–104, 139–140, 145–146, 158–159, 161, 191–195, cited in Newman, L.M. (Ed.) *Men's Ideas, Women's Realities*, pp. 254–255.

5 WEIU, *The Public Schools and Women in Office Work*, Chapter on 'Wages', especially p. 114.

6 Davies, M. *Woman's Place is at the Typewriter*, p. 79.

7 Palmer, A. (1916) 'Letter to the Editor', *New York Times*, 16 May, reprinted in Janeway (Ed.) (1973) *Women, Their Changing Roles*, New York, Arno Press, p. 58.

8 Smith, M.J. (1916) 'Letter to the Editor', *New York Times*, 24 May, reprinted in Janeway, *Women, Their Changing Roles*, p. 58.

9 Ibid.

10 Woods, R.A. and Kennedy, A.J. (1913) *Young Working Girls: A Summary of Evidence from Two Thousand Social Workers*, Boston, Houghton-Mifflin Co., p. 27, quoted in Weiss, J. 'Education for Clerical Work', p. 68.

11 Weiss, J. 'Education for Clerical Work', pp. 75, 79.

12 Latimer, J.F. (1958) *What's Happened to our High Schools?*, Washington DC, Public Affairs Press, pp. 35–36, 145–146.

13 Weiss, J. 'Education for Clerical Work', p. 69.

14 Van Denburg, J.K. (1911) *Causes of the Elimination of Students in Public Secondary Schools of New York City*, New York, Teachers College, Columbia University, pp. 55–57; Department of the Interior, USBE (US Bureau of Education), (1917)

'The Public School System of San Francisco California', *Bulletin 1917*, 46, Washington, DC, GPO, Table 172, p. 516.

15 Holmes, Mrs J. (1915) 'Vocational Opportunities in the Department Store', 16 November, Women in Industry Lecture Series, papers of the NYCBVI, B-3, Box 1, Folder 9, Schlesinger Library, Radcliffe College.

16 Snedden, D. (1920) *Vocational Education*, New York, The MacMillan Company, p. 192.

17 Silverstone, R. (1976) 'Office Work for Women: An Historical Review', 18, No. 1, *Business History*, January, p. 108.

18 (1912) *Life and Labor*, October, p. 293, in the Papers of the NWTUL (National Women's Trade Union League) and Its Principal Leaders, microfilm edition, Schlesinger Library, Radcliffe College.

Part 1 Conclusions

By the time the National Commission on Federal Aid to Vocational Education had convened to discuss policy and future directions in vocational education for young people, (1914), the curricula, lobbies, and competing prescriptions for young women had been shaped. These prescriptions are historically salient because they served to mirror the complex attitudes held by and about women in relation to family life and the work world. As Anne Firor Scott noted, in a period of upheaval and change, complex attitudes reflect various degrees of feminism and traditionalism, often operating side by side. Certainly, within the women's vocational education movement this was true. Women – mainly middle class – representing different agendas formed loose advocacy groups within and between progressive-era organizations to influence the direction of vocational education in the short run and women's place in society in the long run.

Empowered by foot dragging and disinterest on the part of men, women generated the rhetoric and prescriptions about women's place with some interesting and significant consequences. For one thing, unlike the men's vocational education movement which produced two or three major spokesmen who were widely quoted, the women's vocational education movement produced *ad hoc* coalitions. There were no grand architects of women's vocational education and the rhetoric as well as the policies and practices reflect the diversity in perspectives and values that attended the Progressive era women's movement.

This does not suggest of course that all wings of the larger movement were represented within the women's vocational training movement. The vocational interests of middle and upper middle class women with access to secondary and higher education were essentially excluded. But the people and organizations that coalesced to support either trade education or home economics, and to ignore commercial education, enjoyed common Progressive Era goals and perspectives. They all believed that women were primarily wives and mothers; they all lamented the ill effects of unregulated industrial employment on the morals and health of workers; they all believed that women had to take responsibility for their own welfare and the welfare of their children and communities. Beyond these basic ideas, however, critical differences in perspective emerged among them. One essential difference defined the controversy between trade education and home economics advocates, and divided the trade education coalition as well: the tension between traditional values and feminist perspectives. Most home economics advocates believed that women and men occupied separate but equal spheres and sex differentiation was an important and desirable aspect of life. Women's power rested in this difference because they could exercise power either through their competent superintendence of homes, or the home extended into the community. In either case, women had a critical role to play in national life, although in the latter circumstance women would play a much more public role.

The moderate trade education advocates, of whom Jane Addams was typical, basically agreed with the supporters of home economics. Women did occupy a separate sphere and they should be trained for it. That did not exclude training for a job however. They acknowledged that young women should be trained for their short tenure in industry given the evidence that many young women were forced by economic necessity to work until marriage. In the case of reverses of fortune, they should be prepared to pick up their role as wage earner after marriage.

More militant trade education advocates had a vision of women's role that more closely resembled the militancy of late nineteenth century women's rights advocates. They believed that separate was clearly not equal, especially in economics. The sex segregated work force and women's position in low paying low skilled jobs was the root of poverty for many families, especially the single parent families. The NWTUL motto was, 'A working wage to guard the home'. Although they paradoxically supported protective legislation, they also believed in and lobbied for equal access to all trades for women.

The differences in perspective held by individuals and organizations in the women's vocational training movement were profound because they prescribed very different roles in the labor market, exclusion and inclusion. Beyond the differences however, the fact that women defined the goals and perspectives of the movement themselves is significant. Progressive-era female activists believed that women had to take care of and be responsible for other women. Women defined vocational education issues in terms of their progressive-era agenda with all its attendant problems: it was class biased and it was a general prescription for gender segregation.

Prescriptions provide insights into the way people view themselves. It seems evident that the women who shaped the discussions about vocational training linked the discussion and the potential outcomes to larger social issues. They did not see themselves making minor decisions about curriculum, but instead as having an influence on social roles and the quality of American life in the long run. These prescriptions, or visions of 'the way it is "spozed" to be' must be placed along side the politics of policy formulation and the practical dimensions of program implementation for us to see their real significance and evaluate their impact on schooling and young women.

Part 2

Politics

Part 2 Introduction – Politics

Political struggles over the formulation of legislation constitutes the second major dimension of the women's vocational education story. Kliebard has recently argued that vocational education policies are mainly significant as symbolic actions rather than concrete means for accomplishing goals.[1] For the loosely coupled groups who formulated national vocation education policy for girls and women *vis à vis* the Smith-Hughes legislation, the salience was both symbolic and concrete. Decisions made about funding for vocational education paved the way for the construction of a home economics empire: a symbolic gesture that cost the American taxpayers a great deal of money.

The quiet battles waged over definitions of vocational training for young women were significant in their implications. Events surrounding the appointment of the commission, control of the commission agenda, and subsequent power plays by the home economics lobby represented open campaigning for a women's agenda. It was one of the first instances in a national setting where women were instrumental in shaping policy about their own education; they perceived the stakes and called on their well developed organizational skills to wage a very explicit campaign.

In the first round of the campaign to the exclusion of home economic advocates, trade education advocates supporting women's right to work in industry, secured two positions designated for women on the Commission On National Aid to Vocational Education established in 1913. Representatives of the home economics lobby were not informed about the Commission and moreover, responded slowly to the legislation when it was introduced to Congress. They were occupied at the time with the Smith-Lever legislation which provided for agricultural extension agents – some of whom could be women – to deliver education and services to rural areas. When the legislation did get their attention, however, they neutralized the trade education lobby's early gains and skillfully secured the place of home economics in the legislation and ultimately in secondary school curriculum.

Domestic feminists expanded their influence in the years when the Smith-Hughes legislation was developed and first implemented (around 1918–1921). They increased their collaborative efforts and became formally organized in the WJCC (Women's Joint Congressional Committee) under the leadership of the League of Women Voters. The WJCC, called by friends 'the most powerful lobby in Washington'[2] included home economics education on its legislative agenda. Although the WJCC never succeeded in ushering home economics legislation through Congress, they were a powerful presence and their endorsement of the issue was significant.

The trade education lobby and specifically the NWTUL (National Women's Trade Union League) was a visible and highly vocal minority who supported economic independence for women and worked to improve the position of women in industry. However, they never enjoyed widespread popular support, and their agenda was generally overshadowed by their domestic feminist sisters' social legislation.

The development of provisions for women in the Smith-Hughes legislation and their subsequent implementation were controlled by trade education advocates and home economic supporters. Home economics overshadowed trade education, with lasting consequences for women's vocational training in the United States. The victory of home economics was symbolically important because it sanctioned sex differentiated curriculum even though the number of women who actually chose home economics was small. The myth that women's place was in the home was validated.

Notes

1 Kliebard, H. (1990) 'Vocational Education as Symbolic Action: Connecting Schooling With the Workplace', *American Educational Research Journal*, 27, 1, pp. 9–26.
2 Lemmons, S.J. (1973) *The Woman Citizen, Social Feminism in the 1920s*, Urbana, University of Illinois Press, p. 57.

5 Feminist Politics and Personalities Influence Smith-Hughes Legislation

The drive to obtain federal aid for secondary schools was a major thrust of the early vocational education movement. Following the failures of the Davis Dolliver Bill in 1910 and the Page-Wilson Bill of 1912, vocational education proponents in Congress succeeded in passing a resolution that provided for the appointment of a national commission.[1] The nine people appointed to the Commission were charged with investigating the subject of national aid to vocational education and making recommendations to Congress no later than June 1 of that year, 1914.[2] The Commission's hearings, their findings which were synthesized in the proposed Smith-Hughes legislation, and the subsequent floor debates over program definitions and funding, constitute a fascinating and significant chapter in the history of vocational training for women. They were significant because they provided a forum for open discussion between people with conflicting perspectives on appropriate vocational programs for young women. Moreover, the dialogue resulted in funding which substantially influenced vocational education programs in schools throughout the United States. The following chapter explores the discussion surrounding the formulation of guidelines for vocational programs for young women and tells the story of the interest groups, personalities, and perspectives which informed the dialogue and subsequent federal policy.

One focus of debate was the issue of home economics in the Commission's findings. Although home economics had been identified with the vocational education movement from its inception, the commission largely by-passed it in its initial recommendations for funding. Why did the commission limit support for the teaching of home economics when it was enjoying unprecedented support? For the answer to this question and the question of how home economics ended up in the final legislation we need to look at the composition of the commission and the interest groups that lobbied both for and against home economics.

Commercial education was virtually ignored by the commission. In the Commission's recommendations there was no funding provided, either for teacher's salaries or teacher training in this area. This is puzzling given the precipitous growth of the female clerical sector during this period. Of all female non-agricultural workers, 9.2 per cent were involved in clerical work in 1910. It is also puzzling given the popularity of business courses in private business schools and colleges.[3] Interest group politics and the biases of Commission members provide insight into these puzzles.

The overriding issue explored in the chapter is the significance of gender issues and feminist politics in the Commission's development, in the progress of the legislation through Congress, and in the early days of Smith-Hughes implementation.

Feminist Politics and Vocational Education:
The Trade Education Lobby

There were two progressive-era organizations that influenced appointments and recommendations made by the National Commission on Vocational Education, the NWTUL, and the Sub-committee on Industrial Education for Women in the NSPIE (National Society for the Promotion of Industrial Education). The NWTUL was clearly more committed to substantive change in the industrial workplace than the women of NSPIE, however both organizations were committed to providing opportunities for women in trade education.

The NWTUL founded in 1903, was one of the most remarkable reform organizations to emerge during the Progressive Era.[4] Robin Miller Jacoby, a NWTUL archivist, characterized it as 'unique among social reform organizations of its day' because of its genuine concern for and dedication to working women's issues, and because of the cross class makeup of the membership.[5] Another recent history notes that, 'League women were committed to changing society by addressing the problems of workers and the urban poor'.[6] Union members made up the bulk of the membership, and according to the League's constitution, union members were to make up the majority of officers in the national and local leagues. The issues that filled the organization's agenda represented an alliance of 'feminist ideals and labor reform'. They included protectionist legislation for female workers, a minimum working wage, union organizing and strike support, and suffrage, because League women felt that the ballot box in the union hall and the ballot box in the town hall were keys to the improvement of conditions for working women.[7] Education was another item on the League's agenda and this included the education of trade union women for effective bargaining and organizing and industrial education for 'working girls'.

Life and Labor, the official journal of the League is an excellent source of information about the League's educational policies and activities. Numerous articles by League leaders such as Alice Henry, Agnes Nestor, Helen Marot, Margaret Dreier Robins and Leonora O'Reilly reflect the strong feminist position the League took on educational equity and the strategies they developed to disseminate their ideas.[8] The League women publicly argued that young women should have access to the same training and educational opportunities as young men because lack of educational opportunites leads to no possibility of employment in skilled trades and a depressed status in the labor market. They strongly objected to offering domestic science in lieu of trade training for girls and argued that it was unjust to differentiate on the basis of sex in an industrial education curriculum. In a major speech to the 1913 biennial meeting, Robins described an incident of sex bias, where boys were being taught elementary physics, mechanics and electricity in the science course of an industrial education curriculum, while girls were being taught the action of alkalies and the removal of stains from clothing. Robins then appealed to the League women to support a policy of equal education in a statement that predicted Title IX of the Educational Amendments:

> Therefore in the interests of our girls one of the first things to be done is to see that women have seats upon every commission appointed to inquire into systems of vocational training, also upon every board, administrative or advisory, which shall help to direct the activities of all our public school systems, whether vocational or academic, or both.[9]

In addition to taking formal positions on boards and commissions, the League women systematically lobbied school districts on behalf of women's vocational training. For example, Agnes Nestor and Emma Steghagen of the Chicago League went to the School Management Committee of Chicago to lobby for gender equity in course offerings and provision of courses on collective bargaining, industrial history, and subjects related to industrial education.[10] They found an ally on that committee in Superintendent Ella Flagg Young who facilitated community relationships and curriculum development in the form of a course in glove making in the Chicago schools.

Similarly, Leonora O'Reilly, Vice President of the New York League, lobbied the New York school system heavily on behalf of trade training for young women. The Manhattan Trade School for Girls, which O'Reilly was associated with for a number of years and which was often cited as a model of trade training for young women, was formally incorporated into the New York School System presumably as a result of work by O'Reilly and others. O'Reilly's reputation as a teacher of trades and strong supporter of vocational education also earned her an invitation to sit on New York City's schools' advisory board on vocational education established in 1915.[11]

In addition to lobbying local districts for trade education programs, Robins and women of the League understood the value of networking. They established contact with the NSPIE and contributed to annual meetings and bulletins. It was that fruitful contact building that facilitated the appointment of Agnes Nestor to the Commission on National Aid to Industrial Education. Through successful network building Robins was able to influence the appointment of Agnes Nestor to the Commission on National Aid to Vocational Education, and establish ties with the NSPIE.

The NSPIE was established in 1906 by vocational education supporters for 'research, writing and action'.[12] The NSPIE included the interests of women from the very beginning: Jane Addams of Chicago's Hull House was on the first executive Board and on the Sub-committee on Industrial Education for Women which was established in 1907. The roster of prominent women on this committee included Florence M. Marshall, director of the Boston Trade School for Girls and a colleague of Charles Prosser's in the Massachusetts State Department of Education, Mary Morton Kehew, president of the WEIU in Boston, and Mary Schenck Woolman, director of the Manhattan Trade School for Girls.[13] This Sub-committee, headed up by Florence Marshall, provided continual visibility for issues relating to women's industrial education through organization bulletins, presentations made at the organization's annual meeting and networking with other organizations such as the NWTUL. It did not want to accept a marginal position in the NSPIE's agenda, nor in vocational education generally. Bulletins and meeting programs indicate that while education for young women was definitely a visible issue, it did not receive equal treatment. Thus the committee met together in 1912 to discuss the organization's policies with regard to women. The result was a set of strongly worded resolutions that addressed organizational structure and resources. They are appreciable indicators of the determination and organizational sophistication of the authors as well as their commitment to gender equity.

First, the committee urged that the vocational training of women be confined to areas that would lead to self support, which eliminated the possibility of 'vocational homemaking', but did not exclude employment in feminine industries such as laundries. Second, they argued that since the 'facts of our present industrial and agricultural life indicate that the work of wage-earning men and wage-earning women largely coincide', the society should allow for an adequate representation of women on the Board of Managers. Third, the Sub-committee recommended the appointment of a committee of five, composed of two men and two women from the Board and the Executive Secretary to work out the details of expanding the Society's work in this area, and they advised that a 'woman assistant to the Executive Secretary be appointed to aid him [Charles Prosser] in carrying out whatever plans', the committee decided. In a fourth resolution the Sub-committee recommended that research on the needs of women in industry and the distribution of women in industry be conducted; that the effects of minimum wage laws be watched closely and that the society establish a 'closer relationship with the Women's Trade Union League ...'.[14]

These resolutions set forth a well defined feminist agenda for the organization. What seems remarkable in retrospect, even given the reform orientation of the organization, was that the resolutions were accepted by the managing board and that Cleo Murtland of the Worcester Trade School for Girls was hired almost immediately to promote and manage issues relating to women's industrial education, both inside and outside the organization. The agenda and resources to back it up represented a significant vote of confidence for the Sub-committee and the general issue of women's education. Murtland turned out to be an excellent choice judging from the record of her accomplishments. She worked with Charles Prosser on a survey of clothing industries in New York City; she wrote and disseminated articles on the subject to other organizations such as the AHEA (American Home Economics Association); and she was instrumental in the appointment of Florence Marshall and Agnes Nestor to the Commission on Federal Aid to Vocational Education.[15]

Charles Prosser, the Executive Secretary of the NSPIE, was an important ally to the Sub-committee on Industrial Education for Women. He supported the Sub-committee in their goals and worked with them to find the funding to hire Cleo Murtland. He collaborated with Murtland in securing the appointment of Marshall and Nestor to the Commission and he conducted research with her on women in industry and trade education.[16] His support for women's trade education was important both for the NSPIE and the Commission.

It is not easy to discern why some men in the vocational education movement were more willing to support expanded work opportunities for women than others. Yet there does seem to be a relationship between interest in social reform and support for opportunities for women. Prosser was a social reform advocate who worked with young people in his role as juvenile judge in Indiana. He later served as President of the Children's Aid Society in New York City, while pursuing an advanced degree at Columbia University.[17] He was genuinely concerned about the problems of working youths, and strongly believed that schools should play an active role in social reform. Moreover, Prosser believed that 'the school climate should ensure that equal opportunity to learn be made available to all students, both male and female'.[18] Given his social reform roots and commitment to equal opportunities for young women and men, it is not surprising that Prosser would have been such a strong supporter of trade education for women, nor is it surprising that he would have found allies in the NWTUL.

The Sub-committee on Industrial Education for Women, with the crucial assistance of Murtland and Prosser after 1913, was an effective voice in the NSPIE. Women in the NSPIE supported the concept of trade education for women in the feminine industries such as power sewing for clothing industries and millinery trades. Although they disagreed with NWTUL members about open access to all trades and industries for women, together, they were an effective lobby in the campaign to extend vocational education beyond domestic science and housekeeping.

Commission Appointments 'Stacking the Deck' for Trade Education

When vocational education leaders celebrated the establishment of the Commission on National Aid to Vocational Education, the question of women's vocational training was not a major consideration. Finding the means to create efficient vocational training without turning schools into factories was the priority, and Commission appointments were bound to influence the scope and categories for funding. The appointments turned out to be a critical issue for women because the original wording of the Commission recommendation theoretically excluded women. That was changed to include the possibility of female appointments and subsequently two women were chosen to sit on the Commission who heavily influenced the recommendations for women. The orchestration of appointments, of course, was the result of collaboration between the NWTUL and the Sub-committee on Women in Industrial Education of the NSPIE. The story of how the National Commission on Federal Aid to Vocational Education ended up with two women who were trade education advocates, and no women who were home economics advocates is a tribute to the organizational skills of the people involved.

Senator Carroll S. Page (R, Vermont) played a key role in the Commission's composition when he suggested to congressional colleagues that the wording of the resolution be changed. 'Would you accept an amendment making it read, "nine persons" instead of nine men?' he queried.[19] His colleagues assented, the resolution was changed, and two women were appointed. He did that because he had received a letter inquiring about the representation of home economics on the Commission – an issue that he saw as critical – and from his perspective, women needed to formulate that policy, not men.

The next key event was the appointment of Charles Prosser, Executive Secretary of the NSPIE to the Commission. Prosser and his assistant, Cleo

Murtland, looked to their own organization for one of the appointments and then turned to Margaret Dreier Robins, a prominent philanthropist, feminist, trade education advocate, and founding member of the NWTUL for the second appointment. Prosser had worked with David Snedden in Massachusetts as the Deputy Commissioner of Education in charge of industrial education prior to taking the position with the NSPIE. Also he had testified before Congress on previous vocational education legislation. He was a recognized and respected voice in the vocational education movement who was willing to use his influence to support trade education for women by proposing the names of women for the Commission.[20]

Cleo Murtland, the assistant secretary to the NSPIE and an aggressive lobbyist for women's industrial education started lobbying for appointments even before the Commission had been finalized. She wrote to Agnes Nestor on January 16th, 1914, and explained that the wording of the congressional resolution had been changed to read 'nine persons' and asked the NWTUL to 'take steps to interest the President in the appointment of women ... at once'.[21]

Margaret Dreier Robins of the NWTUL was approached by Prosser in January as a potential member of the Commission. Dreier wrote to Prosser and thanked him for including her name on the list of potential appointees but declined. She went on to urge Prosser's support for the appointment of a working woman's representation on the Commission – 'no one knows better than you and the National Society for the Promotion of Industrial Education that women are entering nearly every trade in increasing numbers, and ... that the working women's point of view should be represented on this National Commission by a trade worker'.[22] Dreier went on to suggest that the particular working woman who would be suited to the role was Agnes Nestor.

The NWTUL was organized for lobbying and they put their machine into motion on this issue. By January 17, the leadership had decided to support Agnes Nestor, a leader in the NWTUL, former glove maker and president of the glove makers union in Chicago. Mary Dreier, president of the New York NWTUL, (and sister to Margaret Dreier Robins), was instrumental in the organized response. On January 17th she telegraphed her sister, Margaret Dreier Robins, in Chicago, urging her support for Agnes Nestor; by January 20th President Wilson had received communications from the NWTUL and several local leagues including those of Boston, New York, Chicago, Baltimore and Denver. A subsequent letter from Robins to a potential supporter for Nestor stated that the Consumer's League had telegraphed President Wilson as well, thus indicating that the networking and lobbying by these women extended beyond the League itself.[23]

The two women who were appointed to the Commission were Agnes Nestor, the NWTUL representative and Florence Marshall, director of the Boston Trade School for Girls and a founding member of the NSPIE. Significantly, Marshall was criticized by Robins as a candidate who was too enamored with the feminine trades. Robins confided in personal correspondence that, 'I do not think that Florence Marshall of the Boston Trade School for Girls and women like her ought to be appointed ...', because they 'have simply gone off into "goo goo" work and have no conception at all of the needs of women workers or of the fundamental principles of education'.[24] Robins clearly favored a progressive stand on the issue of women in the trades and was hoping to see that translated into legislation and funding.

Charles Prosser and Cleo Murtland of the NSPIE and the leaders of the NWTUL carefully engineered the appointments of women to the Commission who would support trade education. Murtland confirmed the instrumental role that she and Prosser had played in a letter she wrote to Agnes Nestor after the appointments were made. She wrote, 'You and Miss Marshall are the women whom the men and women of this Society worked for ... The appointments came as a result of a list presented to the President by this Society which I hope to have an opportunity to explain to you sometime'.[25]

There were at least three key factors in the successful engineering of Commission appointments. Prosser's leadership in the vocational education movement lent strength to his recommendations. The NWTUL's leadership was well known and influential in progressive reform circles, especially Margaret Dreier Robins.[26] The combined effect of their stature and the very quick mobilization of support from the feminist network were important considerations in the President's choice of appointees.

Although specific historical evidence is elusive, it also seems probable that supporters of home economics and the other major area of vocational education for women, commercial education, were not consulted or asked to submit names to the President for consideration for appointment. Thus, the only two women on the Commission, along with a key male figure, were strong supporters of trade education for women, a fact that would influence Commission recommendations.

Commission Hearings

Florence Marshall and Charles Prosser of NSPIE, and Agnes Nestor of the NWTUL, worked full-time for approximately two months in the Spring of 1914, along with the other two full-time members of the Commission, John A. Lapp, former Secretary of the Indiana Commission on Industrial Agricultural Education, and Charles H. Winslow, a member in 1906 of the Massachusetts Commission on Industrial Education.[27] Marshall and Nestor's primary goal was to create a workable plan for vocational education that included a strong provision for women's trade education. The basic issue facing them in the commission proceedings was a conflict over the place of home economics in vocational education. From Nestor's perspective:

> Miss Florence Marshall and I foresaw difficulties when we found that some of the men wished to give girls more domestic science than opportunity to learn trades ... We felt that if domestic science were allowed the greater appropriation, it would be too easy to push all the girls into that field and not give them the technical training they were likely to find themselves in need of.[28]

Nestor was committed to absolutely equal opportunities for boys and girls, and she publicly argued that no more technical schools be opened unless the same provisions were made for girls as boys.[29]

In another example of superb orchestration and collaboration, Nestor and Marshall took charge of Commission hearings when the subject of vocational training for young women was discussed. Through carefully worded questions they were able to elicit supportive testimony from representatives of three of the four major women's groups in the country who were interested in vocational education, NWTUL, NSPIE, and the GFWC (General Federation of Women's Clubs). One of the lynchpins of Marshall and Nestor's argument was that all young women would profit from home economics as part of general education but home economics should not be a substitute for vocational education. Laura Drake Gill, a founding member of the NSPIE, testified that, '... all women should have an occupation that would provide for self support, and that all women should make their contribution to the world's work'.[30] She went on to argue that home economics belonged to the category called general education, and that home economics should include training for household trades that would lead to jobs.

Leonora O'Reilly, of the NWTUL, gave the most colorful and the most passionate statement recorded in the Congressional Hearings. O'Reilly was a second generation union activist, a committed socialist, a friend of Agnes Nestor, and devout supporter of equity issues. She was a charismatic figure who has been described as 'one of the most unforgettable NWTUL activists', who 'attracted people like a magnet'.[31] Her testimony stands out because of the power of her language and the fact that she was speaking to some fairly conservative congressmen who believed that women belonged at home. There were a number of important points that O'Reilly made during her testimony to support trade education. She argued that education should not discriminate between boys and girls, stating, 'If a girl can drive a nail better than a boy don't call her a tomboy for doing ... [it] And if a boy can sew on a button better than a girl, why, let him sew on his buttons'. Extending this concept of equity to the workplace, she went on to say, 'why should we not get out of our head this idea that women are made for that kind of work and men are made for the other kind. If a man is a better cook let him cook, and if a woman can do better work on the farm let her do it'.

When questioned by Marshall about the importance of home economics in a young woman's education O'Reilly was equally forthright. O'Reilly responded vehemently that:

> So many of us have not anything like homes ... and if we do make the mistake to get married we go back to the mill afterwards to help support the children which may come and can not be supported by the wages that are paid in the mills.... No, I think it is a very great mistake if you think there should be no special training in this vocational work except to fit women to be cooks for other women who do not want to do their cooking and that is largely what it means.[32]

Marshall knew that O'Reilly and other members of the NWTUL felt strongly about the issue of home economics and in particular objected to the prospect of training young women in schools for employment as domestics.

O'Reilly's testimony was significant because she could speak eloquently from first hand experience about the life and oppression of working class women. Her mother had struggled to support the family as a garment maker and Leonora had left school at age eleven to work in a collar factory.[33] Since she had first attended the Manhattan Trade School and then worked as a teacher she felt strongly that education would help women to take their place alongside men in all phases of industry. She elaborated on this point saying that over specialization in industry had created 'dead end' jobs for women who might be stuck sewing the same seam or part of a seam for a number of years. Vocational training that taught women to make a whole garment or perform a number of functions would help them to compete with men in industry.[34]

The third organization to speak on behalf of women's vocational education, and the only organization representing an alternative to trade education was the GFWC. Mrs Horace Towner, the wife of Congressman Towner (R, Iowa) spoke for the GFWC, and it was evident from her testimony that she had not been briefed on the specific issues involved in the Commission's work. Her comments were vague, and they did not reflect the GFWC's keen interest in home economics. For example, when Marshall questioned her about the GFWC's position on the training of girls who must earn a living, Mrs Towner responded that the, 'General Federation is interested in every thing of that sort'. When she was asked to what extent she thought home economics should be part of general education or vocational education, she replied, 'That is a very big question'. Nestor pressed her further rephrasing the question to: 'Do you not think the home economics ought to be part of a general education?' Mrs Towner finally replied, 'yes'.[35] The significance of Mrs Towner's testimony was that it helped to strengthen the hand of the trade education advocates in formulating the legislation.

Commission members were part of the recorded testimony and there was support for home economics on the Commission. For example Senator Page, a basically conservative country gentleman, testified that, 'the Almighty ... has ordained that woman do the housework and the man do the work which he does'. Although he professed a belief that women should be given equal opportunities with men, he also thought that equal opportunities did not mean 'putting a woman into man's work in the field, in the stable, or in the hide house'.[36] He made a point of distinguishing between rural and urban needs in the Commission hearings, arguing that young women in rural states such as Georgia, Iowa, and Vermont look forward to their roles as homemakers. For them vocational training in the trades would be impractical, whereas home economics for the keeper of the farm home would be very practical.

Unlike home economics which had at least two spokespersons on the Commission, commercial education was virtually ignored. The only person to address the topic was the Secretary of Commerce, William Cox Redfield. He opposed funding for commercial education, contending that the, 'Need is far greater for the training of the mechanic than it is for the training of the office clerk'. He was speaking of 'The office man', as he put it and at no point discussed the advent of women into the clerical force or the growth in the clerical work force.[37]

Support for commercial education might have come from the Business Education Association. However, the relationship between business educators and vocational educators was tenuous at best. As Janice Weiss explains in her thesis on education for clerical work, the business education community did not want to be identified with vocational education; they preferred to be associated with professional schools and courted 'the acceptance of academic educators'.[38] Vocational educators charged that commercial education was not practical enough to qualify as vocational education. Thus by mutual agreement commercial education was not proposed for funding.

In addition to the omission of oral testimony, the people who sat on the Commission did not address the topic in the published hearings. Neither Marshall nor Nestor brought up the topic of commercial education, and it seems evident that it was a deliberate omission. It may seem curious that during a period of rapid growth in the number of women in office service that Marshall and Nestor would have failed to recognize the potential significance of this work. However, it is congruent with the perspectives of the NSPIE and NWTUL. They both classified commercial work as 'professional,' similar to teaching. In both of their organizations' publications the subject of commercial education and office workers was virtually ignored. Since both organizations were committed to the advancement of women in industry and the promotion of industrial education, commercial education was outside the purview of their stated interests.

Commission Recommendations: A Vote For Industrial Education

Commission recommendations presented to Congress in June of 1914 held no surprises for close observers of the Commission. Funding for home economics and commercial education was restricted while agriculture education and training for the trades and industries were generously supported. Funding for home economics was limited to teacher training, which excluded salaries for teachers and supervisory personnel, except in agricultural education. There was no funding for commercial education for either teacher salaries or teacher training.

The Commission discussed the limitation of funding for home economics and commercial education in its report, stating that the criterion for receiving federal aid would be acknowledged need: 'National grants should be given to the States only for those forms of vocational education where there is an acknowledged widespread need that is not now being met'.[39] The report went on to explain that the Commission's treatment of home economics was based on two key ideas. The first was that home economics would be an important part of every girl's education and thus should be classified as general education rather than vocational, a strategic point for the trade education advocates. The second was that, 'so far as the towns and cities are concerned, general training for the home is being rapidly developed . . . in the absence of national grants [it] will not be neglected'.[40]

Commercial education was eliminated from funding based on the same principle of 'acknowledged need'. According to the Commission findings, commercial education was already being provided for in schools. Moreover, there was no 'great scarcity of trained workers of this kind'. Although there may not have been a scarcity of trained workers in this area, it was one of the fastest growing occupations for women. In the years between 1900 and 1910, the increase was 133.19 per cent.[41]

The cornerstone of the argument for excluding funding for home economics and commercial education, that they were already being provided for whereas agriculture and trade and industrial education were not, is not supported by statistics from the period. Trade and industrial courses were not offered in many schools, however agriculture courses, commercial education and home economics were offered in about the same number, according to a federal government survey. A more plausible explanation and one that this chapter has argued is that the trade education lobby on the Commission ensured the inclusion of a strong vote for women's industrial training, the relative exclusion of home economics, and the complete exclusion of commercial education.

The organizational skills of the women involved were superb. The NSPIE and the NWTUL were organized for legislative advocacy and political action. They successfully bid for seats on the Commission, orchestrated the hearings and testimony and negotiated with the agrarian interests over home economics in the rural schools. What they accomplished, for a brief moment in history, was a symbolic statement about the right of young women to education and work that was comparable to that of young men. In the United States, this issue would not come up in legislation for another fifty years.

The group of women who gathered under the umbrella of vocational education and trade education represent a spectrum of feminist and traditional perspectives. The issue of race, as is evident in this chapter was not raised in the government hearings and was not evident in the published rhetoric of the time. We can conclude, accurately so, that for the women of the NSPIE and NWTUL education for blacks and non-whites was not an issue they were concerned about and the absence of attention was probably based on racism. The phenomenon of middle-class reforms imposed on working class sisters, social protectionism, is a criticism that has been directed at the large sorority of feminine and feminist reformers of the Progressive Era. It is a criticism that fits and doesn't fit the women who were forging national policy in vocational training for young women. The concept of equity proposed by the women of the NWTUL was fairly radical for the period. The League women focused their attention on working class girls and hence were proposing a class based reform, yet it was working class women whose roots were in industry and sincerely wanted the lives of their little sisters to improve.

The women of the NSPIE were in general more conservative and found it easier to discuss feminine trades and other compromises which supported labor market segmentation and differential access to education. Yet both groups and the two women who were responsible for the Commission recommendations were immovable in their belief that women belonged in the labor market and that public education had the responsibility to take that seriously. This belief was not widely accepted in a period when women's role in the home and in the work place was considered problematic. The events which unfolded after the Commission presented its recommendations provide historical evidence of the extent to which that was problematic.

Notes

1 US Congress, Public Resolution No. 16, 63rd Congress, 2nd Session, Senate Joint Resolution 5, cited in *Report of Commission on National Aid to Vocational Education* 2 volumes, House Document 1004, 63rd Congress, 2nd Session, *Congressional Record*, 9537, 9611.
2 US Congress, Public Resolution No. 16, 63rd Congress.
3 Rotella, E.J. (1981) *From Home to Office, US Women at Work, 1870–1930*, Ann

Arbor, UMI Research Press, p. 32; Weiss, J. (1978) Ed.D. dissertation 'Educating for Clerical Work: A History of Commercial Education in the US Since 1850', Cambridge, Harvard Graduate School of Education, p. 6; for the history of federal legislation see Hawkins, L., Prosser, C.A. and Wright, J.C. (1951) *Development of Vocational Education*, Chicago, American Technical Society, pp. 396–399.

4 Payne, E.A. (1988) *Reform, Labor and Feminism*, Urbana, University of Illinois Press, p. 1.

5 Jacoby, R.M. 'Introduction', Microfilm Edition of the Papers of the NWTUL (National Women's Trade Union League) and Its Principal Leaders, p. 11.

6 op. cit., Payne, p. 1.

7 Jacoby, R.M. 'Introduction', Microfilm Edition of the Papers of the NWTUL and Its Principal Leaders, p. 28.

8 See Dye, N.S. (1980) *As Equals and As Sisters, Feminism, the Labor Movement and the Women's Trade Union League of New York*, Columbia, University of Missouri Press; Jacoby, R.M. Notes for Microfilm Edition of the Papers of the NWTUL and Its Principal Leaders; and *Life and Labor*, Volumes 1 through 12 in Microfilm Edition of the Papers of the NWTUL and Its Principal Leaders.

9 Henry, A. (1954) 'Vocational Training Symposium', p. 43.

10 Nestor, A. *Women's Labor Leader*, pp. 144–145; Henry, A. (1914) 'Chicago Conference of Trade Unionists', *Life and Labor*, November, p. 327, in Papers of the NWTUL.

11 Letter from Palmer, A.E. to O'Reilly, L., 28 October 1915, in Leonora O'Reilly papers, Reel 10, Papers of the NWTUL.

12 Robins, M.D. (1910) 'Industrial Education for Women', NSPIE *Proceedings of the Third Annual Meeting*, Bulletin 10, March, 78.

13 NSPIE, (1908) *Circular of Information, Constitution, State Branches, Officers and Members*, Bulletin 7, p. 7.

14 (1914) 'Report of the Committee on Women's Work', Report of the Secretary, NSPIE (National Society for the Promotion of Industrial Education), *Proceedings Seventh Annual Meeting*, Grand Rapids, March, pp. 156–162, 251, 253, 258.

15 Murtland, C. and Prosser, C. (1915) 'Conciliation, Arbitration and Sanitation in the Dress and Waist Industry of New York', US Department of Labor *Bulletin 145*, Appendix I, passim; Greenwood, K.B.L. 'A Philosophic Rationale for Vocational Education: Contributions of Charles A. Prosser and His Contemporaries from 1900 to 1917', p. 180.

16 Prosser's role in Commission appointments is alluded to in correspondence between Murtland and Nestor in Agnes Nestor papers, Reel 115, Papers of the NWTUL; see also 'Report of the Secretary', NSPIE, *Proceedings Seventh Annual Meeting*, pp. 251–253.

17 Greenwood, K.L. 'A Philosophic Rationale For Vocational Education', p. 180.

18 Prosser, C. (1911) 'Commentary', NSPIE, *Proceedings of the Fourth Annual Meeting, Boston, Mass.*, January, pp. 49–50.

19 Allinson, M. (1914) *The Public Schools and Women in Office Service*, Boston, WEIU (Women's Educational and Industrial Union), p. 2.

20 Greenwood, K.L.B. (1978) Ph.D. dissertation 'A Philosophic Rationale for Vocational Education; Contributions of Charles A. Prosser and His Contemporaries From 1900 to 1917, Volume Two'. University of Minnesota, p. 247.

21 Letter from Murtland, C. to Nestor, A. 16 January 1914, in Agnes Nestor Papers, Microfilm Edition of the Papers of the NWTUL and Its Principal Leaders, Reel 115.

22 Letter from Prosser, C.A. to Robins, M.D. 27 January 1914, and letter from Robins, M.D. to Prosser, C.A. 30 January 1914 in MDR (Margaret Dreier

Robins) papers, University of Florida Libraries, Microfilm Edition of the Papers of the NWTUL and Its Principal Leaders, Reel 23.

23 Letter from Robins, M.D. to Miss Gillespie, 20 January 1914, MDR Papers, Reel 23.

24 Telegram noted in letter from Robins, M.D. to Dreier, M. Dated 17 January 1914, in MDR papers, Reel 23.

25 Letter from Murtland, C. to Nestor, A. 18 February 1914, in Microfilm Edition of the Papers of the NWTUL and Its Principal Leaders, Reel 115.

26 For information on Robins, M.D. see James, E., James, J. and Boyer, P. (Eds) *Notable American Women*, Cambridge, Belknap Press, 2, pp. 179–181.

27 Greenwood, K.L. 'A Philosophic Rationale for Vocational Education', p. 179; Members of the Commission Appointed by President Wilson were; Senator H. Smith, Georgia; Senator C.S. Page, Vermont; Representative D.N. Hughes, Georgia; Representative S.D. Fess, Ohio; J.A. Lapp, Director of Indiana Bureau of Legislative Information; Miss F.M. Marshall, director Manhattan Trade School; Miss A. Nestor, President International Glove Workers' Union; C.A. Prosser, Secretary NSPIE (National Society for the Promotion of Industrial Education); C.H. Winsow, special agent, Bureau of Labor Statistics.

28 Nestor, A. *Woman Labor Leader*, p. 151.

29 Ibid., p. 152.

30 US Congress, *Report of the Commission on National Aid to Vocational Education*, 2, Hearings, p. 137.

31 Wertheimer, B.M. (1977) *We Were There, The Story of Working Women in America*, New York, Pantheon, pp. 276–279.

32 US Congress, *Report of the Commission on National Aid to Vocational Education*, 2, Hearings, pp. 194–195.

33 For information on O'Reilly see Lagemann, E.C. (1979) *A Generation of Women, Education in the Lives of Progressive Reformers*, Cambridge, Harvard University Press, pp. 89–114; and Leonora O'Reilly papers in Microfilm Edition of The Papers of the NWTUL and Its Principal Leaders.

34 US Congress, *Report of the Commission on National Aid to Vocational Education*, Hearings, p. 194.

35 US Congress, *Report of the Commission on National Aid to Vocational Education*, Hearings, pp. 205, 206.

36 US Congress, *Report of the Commission on National Aid to Vocational Education*, Hearings, p. 203.

37 US Congress, *Report of the Commission on National Aid to Vocational Education*, Hearings, p. 202.

38 US Congress, *Report of the Commission on National Aid to Vocational Education*, 2, Hearings, pp. 38–54.

39 Ibid., p. 41.

40 US Congress, *Report of the Commission on National Aid to Vocational Education*, 2, Hearings, pp. 38–54.

41 Rotella, E.J. (1981) *From Home to Office, US Women at Work, 1870–1930*, Ann Arbor, UMI Research Press, p. 32; Weiss, J. (1978) Ed.D. dissertation 'Educating for Clerical Work: A History of Commercial Education in the US since 1850', Cambridge, Harvard Graduate School of Education, p. 6; for the history of federal legislation see Hawkins, L., Prosser, C.A. and Wright, J.C. (1951) *Development of Vocational Education*, Chicago, American Technical Society, pp. 396–399.

6   Congressional Politics and the Home Economics Lobby

Whereas the trade education advocates dominated decisions about vocational education for young women in Commission preceedings, the home economics lobby took over when the Commission recommendations were presented to Congress as the Smith–Hughes Bill. The GFWC (General Federation of Women's Clubs), the AHEA (American Home Economics Association) and a handful of Congressmen were instrumental in changing funding provisions for home economics in the Smith–Hughes Bill. This increased funding provision was a significant factor in the future of vocational education for women. This chapter will focus on the changes made in the legislation and the individuals and organization responsible for the changes.

In the Commission recommendations presented to Congress by Senator Page, home economics funding was limited and commercial education was given no funding for teaching and training. When the bill went into the House of Representatives Education Committee, however, home economics funding was increased to provide for teaching and teacher training. Representative Fess, of Ohio, a member of the Commission a supporter of home economics, reported on the floor of Congress that when the committee took up the matter of home economics the argument was pretty strongly pressed that we ought to recognize home economics teaching as well as home economics training. He indicated that the change had been made, 'upon the representation of a group of women who knew the situation pretty well'. These women were representatives of the GFWC, a conservative women's organization dedicated to a number of progressive reform causes that included the dissemination of home economics in schools.[1]

The role of the GFWC in the legislative change was indicated in the 'Legislation' column of the March 1915 *Federation Bulletin*. The columnist stated that the club women who were experienced along the lines of home economics had advised them that it was a 'matter of some doubt', whether or not the proposed Smith–Hughes legislation met the needs of home economics. She went on to note that it was fortunate, given the objections, that there was time for further consideration of the legislation.[2] A subsequent article in the March 1916 *Bulletin* indicated that the bill had been amended in the house to the approval of all parties and that the legislation now covered, 'Agricultural, Industrial and Home Economics lines in about equal proportions'.[3]

One organization that was conspicuously absent in the drive to increase home economics funding was the AHEA. The AHEA position on Smith-Hughes was discussed in the organization's publication, the *American Home Economic Journal*: two separate articles indicated no intention to lobby for more home economics funding. An April 1916 article attempted to define the difference between general home economics and vocational home economics. A subsequent June 1916 article by the chairman of the legislation committee indicated that from her perspective the 'original commission felt that most states have excellent provision for the training of teachers for the general phases of household economics or household arts', and that the funding levels in the proposed Smith-Hughes legislation were sufficient to promote the general teaching of the subject.[4] It seems curious that the legislative department of the home economics professional association would take a stand that was clearly counter productive to their goals. The evidence suggests there were two possible considerations. One is that the AHEA legislative chairman did not understand the importance of funding. Furthermore, it is evident in the *American Home Economics Journal* issues of the period that the Association was preoccupied with the Smith-Lever Bill which provided for the equivalent of agricultural extension agents for home economics.[5] The Smith-Lever legislation had the potential to affect a large number of farm people of all ages, including young farm women, and the AHEA women concentrated heavily on it.

AHEA's absence in the lobbying process did not significantly affect the outcome of the Smith-Hughes legislation, however. The GFWC was very effective in their drive to influence funding levels. The question of why the GFWC was so interested in home economics leads to a discussion of the organization's orientation and philosophy, and a comparison of the Federation with the NWTUL (National Women's Trade Union League).

The General Federation of Women's Clubs

The GFWC was an organization that boasted a membership of nearly one million members and forty-six state federations by 1910. The organization was an outgrowth of the Sorosis Club started by Jane Cunningham Croly in 1868 as an alternative to militant feminist organizations seeking suffrage, economic independence and political power.[6] Unlike the NWTUL, the organization was middle and upper middle class in its composition and unapologetic about its class identification. Articles in the *The General Federation Bulletin* frequently referred to those women who were 'less fortunate' as their little sisters.[7] This class consciousness was not lost on the Federation's critics and it was a major issue that distinguished it from the NWTUL, which was numbered among its critics. 'Margaret Dreier Robins pointed out that membership in the General Federation was so elitist that not one of the six million working class women was represented at the [1908 NWTUL] Boston Biennial'.[8]

That the Federation was concerned about working women and their lives is evident in their co-sponsorship of the massive *Report on Condition of Women and Child Wage-Earners in the United States*, the numerous articles on women in industry included in the *Federation Bulletin*, and the establishment of its Committee on Industry and Women.[9] Yet, the major emphasis on the GFWC's work was the protection of women from the harmful influences and conditions of industry that destroyed health and forced young women 'into immoral lives'. From the perspective of the GFWC, it was far more desirable for young women to go into domestic service than to pursue a career in industry. The anti-industry bias was so pronounced that the chairman of the Committee on Industry and Women for the GFWC, Rheta Childe Dorr felt obligated to defend her Committee in a 1905 Bulletin, stating:

> The general impression seems to be that something ought to be done to check the migration from home to factory, shop, and office. It is not the object of this committee to oppose this idea! ... [10]

The Committee and the organization were interested in protecting women and the home from the negative influences which threatened both and the advent of women into industry was viewed as a problem rather than as an opportunity.

The women of the Federation were domestic feminists. Recalling the discussion of domestic feminism in Chapter 2, domestic feminism was predicated on the belief that women's true vocation was homemaking but that twentieth century homemaking extended into the neighborhood schools and municipal and federal government. Protecting the home from the harmful effects of industrialization and urbanization was the peculiar province of women;

> If the natural guardians of the the home pay little heed or give an uncertain warning of the dangers threatening the welfare of our home, school and national life, who shall prepare for battle against evil, in all its hideous forms?[11]

Home economics was the means by which young women would be prepared for their vocation; schools were the institutions that were destined to provide it. Home economics, as it was conceived of by Ellen Richards and her predecessors in the AHEA and GFWC, was the medium through which the socialization of new generations of municipal house-keepers would be accomplished, and ultimately it held the ulimate promise of uplifting civilization, through the physical, moral, and mental improvement of the race.[12]

Apart from instilling a love of homemaking and an appreciation of municipal housekeeping, home economics also held the key to the 'servant problem'. Between 1910 and 1920 the number of domestic servants declined by approximately 25 per cent.[13] Federation women lamented both the decline in numbers and the low skills that young domestic servants brought to their employment. As this problem was expressed by one club woman:

> In any discussion of the standards of home life in the Middle West, a serious and perplexing problem thrusts itself in the front – the homemaking-housekeeping – domestic-service problem. It is serious because it threatens, especially in the cities, to substitute apartments in a family hotel for the old-fashioned home. It is perplexing because, working women are generally unwilling to accept domestic service as a means of

gaining a living, and, most of all because the woman heads of families are doing little to improve the situation.[14]

The solution to this problem lay in home economics which promised to raise the status of domestic work by making it more 'scientific', providing training for young women who would be domestic servants, especially the immigrants who 'brought low standards of living into the American household' and to educate the future homemakers so they could manage their homes and servants more efficiently and ultimately spend their time on municipal housekeeping and child rearing.[15]

The GFWC promoted home economics in public schools with a missionary zeal throughout the first two decades of the twentieth century. 'Salvation through scientific investigation and cooperation', in the advancement of home economics was the goal.[16] 'Everywhere the women have been instrumental in establishing courses and departments of domestic science in all sorts of educational institutions from the vacation school to the university', declared one mid-western club woman.[17] 'The advent of home economics into the public schools is in many cases due largely to the assistance of women's clubs', exclaimed a representative of the AHEA.[18] Thus the Federation's interest in the Smith-Hughes legislation and its support for the inclusion of home economics was very much in keeping with their general philosophy of woman's role as homemaker, mother, and municipal housekeeper, as well as with their ambivalence about women in industry.

It is clear that many women of the Federation believed that young women's education should differ from young men's. One home economics supporter argued in the *Federation Bulletin* that the curriculum then taught in schools was inconsistent with the goals of young women's education. Rather than learning about Greek Art and Latin verbs, young women should learn about hygienic clothing and modified milk; rather than learning about the changing republics of Central America, they should learn about household bacteriology, personal hygiene and prevention of disease.[19] Unlike the NWTUL, which extended the concept of equity to curriculum offerings, the GFWC supported equity in funding but wanted young women educated for their future roles as homemakers rather than wage earners; thus it supported sex differentiated curriculum.

Congressional Support

The Federation's success in raising the funding level of home economics could not have been achieved without the sympathetic help of some Congressmen who wanted to see home economics instituted in the schools as the mainstay of vocational education for young women. These legislators argued eloquently and persuasively to their Congressional colleagues that the funding of home economics would improve the status of American homes, both urban and rural, and discourage competition from women in the workplace. Senator Page was a particularly strong advocate of home economics who linked the demise of the American family to the lack of training for young women. His remarks to the Senate introducing the Smith-Hughes legislation provide an excellent example of his perspective which attributed incredible results to the teaching of home economics:

> The statistics show that 600,000 infants under 2 years of age annually terminate their little span of life and that 5,000,000 people are every year made ill by preventable diseases. . . . With the knowledge which I believe this bill will give, a large percentage of these 600,000 infants could be saved and the physical standards of those who reach mature years be immeasurably raised. Without this knowledge thousands of homes will be wrecked, thousands of lives ruined, and hundreds of thousands made unhappy for no other reason than that the homekeepers of our country have no adequate training in that most important of all duties, the making of a well-regulated, intelligently-conducted household. . . . It is coming to be more and more realized that we must give to our girls a training different from that with which we now provide them if crime, disease, divorce, and race suicide are not to continue to increase. . . .[20]

Senator Moore, (R, Pennsylvania) and Representative Towner (R, Iowa) also felt strongly about the advent of women into the work place, especially the industrial work place. They both argued that training for home making was a much more appropriate vocational training than industrial training. Moore stated fervently to an apparently appreciative congressional audience that he 'would not permit a girl to work in a mill', if he could have his way. He continued, saying that, 'many of the girls of this country are being weaned away from the home life, which they ought to learn to respect, and encouraged to go into the mills, factories, and foundries with, if you please, the purpose of competing with men . . .'[21] Similarly, Representative Towner, whose wife testified on behalf of the GFWC during the Commission hearing on federal aid for vocational education, complained that,

> under present conditions the girls' education is more directed to the making of school-teachers or shop girls than to the making of homemakers. . . . It will benefit the whole scheme of home-making and home-keeping if you elevate the home in the mind of the girl who thinks too much about becoming a shop girl, or a factory worker, rather than of going to the home and becoming a mother . . .[22]

In the opinion of these men, and the Congressional audience who applauded Moore's comments, women did not belong in the work place, and schools ought not to encourage their presence by offering them training.

Support for teaching home economics in the schools also came from rural life advocates in Congress who viewed the exodus of young women from country to city as a threat to rural life. Their fears were realistic as subsequent 1920 census data reported in the *New York Times* indicated: 'larger numbers of women than of men are leaving farms in search of more lucrative fields of endeavor'.[23] The solution to this problem lay in providing monies for agricultural education that would emphasize home economics and the farm home, as well as crops in the field. Senator Moore of Pennsylvania, for example, suggested that, 'Each state should induce its young women as well as young men to stay on the farm', and Representative Sloan of Nebraska argued that young farm women who were trained in home economics could not only become the happy superintendents of farm homes but would serve as an attraction to young farm men.[24]

It is significant that the majority of remarks on vocational education for young women offered during floor discussions in Congress concentrated on home economics: there were no strong supporters of trade education, and there were no advocates of commercial education. Moreover, after the Federation women voiced their objections to the legislation, (with no funding for home economics teaching), access to the House of Representatives Committee on Education was still available through Representative Towner. Representative Towner was a vocal advocate of home economics for young women as was Representative Fess, another member of the House Education Committee. Both were instrumental in changing the legislation.

The victory for home economics that was won through the cooperative efforts of the GFWC and the interested Congressmen was important for several reasons. It ensured the place of home economics as the main focus of vocational education for young women, and it legitimized the concept of sex differentiated education programs. Moreover, it served as an indicator that the ideal that woman's place was in the home was still a fundamental premise and social organizer for a large group of men and women. The right for women to work was not going to go unchallenged. The conflict generated over home economics in the Smith-Hughes legislation, and the challenge to traditional definitions of woman's place were as important as the victory, however. The position of the NWTUL and the NSPIE (National Society for the Promotion of Industrial Education) represented a growing minority of women who recognized and accepted the fact that many women worked in industry and believed that options for advancement, better working conditions, and more equitable pay scales should be guaranteed by educational as well as regulatory provisions.

Differing perspectives on the question of vocational education for young women reflected the diverse directions that feminism took during the progressive period. The GFWC and the NWTUL shared a belief that social reform must be instigated by women and that women occupied a special place in society. They both wanted to see the status and conditions of women improved and they shared concern over the evils of industry; long hours, poor working conditions, low wages, and inadequate child care facilities. They were equally concerned with infant mortality, over-worked mothers, child labor, and the effects of poor wages which allegedly drove women into prostitution. They were all products of the social reform school which saw women as the saviors of other women in the short run and society in the long run.

Their differences, however, were as significant as what they shared in common. The women of the trade education lobby, the NSPIE and the NWTUL, were closely aligned to working class people and their problems. They accepted the reality that many women would work for a substantial period of their lives, that without training they would not earn a decent wage and that they could not advance from their low level position in the labor force. Economic power through better and more equitable training, higher wages, and union organization were the keys to poverty, infant mortality, and the host of social problems that concerned women, and thus vocational training for young women was a critical issue.

The home economics enthusiasts focused on the home as the center of women's lives. They did not accept women's role in the work force as a given but as a temporary condition following graduation from high school or in the event of unforeseen reverses. The feminine industries and domestic service were the ones for young women to turn to under those circumstances, where women would be protected from the evils of industry while preparing themselves for their roles as keepers of the home and nurturers of the family. They did not see economic independence as a significant goal, but were more concerned with supporting and uplifting the traditional sphere of women. In terms of sex segregation in education the lobbies supported distinctly opposite points of view. The trade education lobby felt that the vocational education of young people should make no distinctions based on sex. The Committee on Women's Work of the NSPIE and the NWTUL were both very clear on this point. Cleo Murtland spoke to this point in the *Journal of Home Economics*, stating, 'It is the very strong desire of the women engaged in the vocational education movement to keep the work for boys and girls one strong unit'.[25] The NWTUL was equally determined about equity as indicated in their 1913 resolution which stated:

> Resolved; That the National Women's Trade Union League urge upon the educational authorities to establish trade and technical and vocational industrial schools in connection with the public schools, and that the course of instruction in such schools include, besides the subjects necessary to trade training, the history of the trades, taught, the history of the evolution of industry, ...; also that all training in such schools be co-educational, the boy and girl studying the same subjects.[26]

In contrast, the home economics lobbies wanted a distinctly feminine vocational education for young women as befitted a woman's ultimate vocation of homemaking. With critical support from Congressmen, the home economics lobby was primarily responsible for the institutionalization of home economics in the comprehensive high school and junior high.

Notes

1 *US Congress, House Committee on Education*, Hearings on Federal Aid for Home Economics, HR 12078 66th Congress, 3rd session, 4 February 1921, p. 3.
2 Blair, K.J. (1980) *The Clubwoman as Feminist, True Womanhood Redefined, 1868–1914*, New York, Holmes and Meier Publishers, Inc., p. 40.
3 See *The General Federation of Women's Clubs Magazine*, for the years 1904–1915. See especially January 1905, p. 116 and July 1911, p. 540.
4 Kinne, H. (1916) 'Terminology and the Smith-Hughes Bill', *The Journal of Home Economics*, April, p. 186.
5 US Congress, 'Report on Condition of Women and Child Wage Earners in the United States', Senate Document 645, 61st Congress, 2nd Session; see (1904) 'The Work of Women's Clubs', *The Federation Bulletin*, January, pp. 44–45.
6 Dorr, R.C. (1905) 'Report on Women in Industry', *The Federation Bulletin*, June, p. 297; (1912) 'Home Economics', *The Federation Bulletin*, September, p. 458.

7   Mears, Mrs D.O. (1910) 'What is Worth While in Club Life', *Federation Bulletin*, p. 26.
8   Harper, I.H. (1909) 'Woman's Broom in Municipal Housekeeping', *The Federation Bulletin*, June, p. 246; see also Blair, K. *The Clubwoman as Feminist*, especially the introduction, p. 1.
9   Hill, J. *Women in Gainful Occupations 1870–1920*, Westport, Greenwood Press, p. 37.
10 Rhodes, E.M. (1905) 'A New Line of Study for Women's Clubs', *The Federation Bulletin*, June, pp. 298–299.
11 Sherman, M.B.K. (1908) 'What Are Club Women Doing for the Home', *The Federation Bulletin*, January, p. 126.
12 Sherman, M.B.K. 'What Are Club Women Doing for the Home', p. 127.
13 Johnson, H.L. (1909) 'Domestic Science in the Schools', *The Federation Bulletin*, November, p. 52.
14 Green, Mrs C.W. (1916) 'Home Economics', *The Federation Bulletin*, January, p. 26.
15 (1915) 'Legislation', *The General Federation of Women's Clubs Magazine*, March, p. 39.
16 (1916) *The General Federation of Women's Clubs Magazine*, March, p. 17.
17 Page, Senator C.H. (2 January 1917) US Congress, *Congressional Record*, 54, 64th Congress, 2nd Session, p. 11467.
18 US Congress, *Congressional Record*, 54, 64th Congress, 2nd Session, 2 January 1917, p. 764.
19 Ibid., pp. 757, 764.
20 (1922) *New York Times*, 'Women Leave the Farm', 30 November reprinted in Janeway, (Ed.), *Women, Their Changing Roles*, New York, Arno Press, p. 127.
21 US Congress, *Congressional Record*, 62nd Congress, 2nd session, p. 11626.
22 Ibid., pp.757, 764.
23 (1922) *New York Times*, 'Women Leave the Farm', 30 November reprinted in Janeway, (Ed.), *Women, Their Changing Roles*, New York, Arno Press, p. 127.
24 US Congress, *Congressional Record*, 62nd Congress, 2nd session, p. 11626.
25 Murtland, C. (1916) 'Aims and Work of the National Society for the Promotion of Industrial Education', *The Journal of Home Economics*, 8, January, 1, p. 10.
26 (1913) 'Fourth Biennial Outlines Work', *Life and Labor*, August, p. 236.

7   Post Smith–Hughes Politics

Following three of years of lobbying by vocational educators and other organizations the Smith-Hughes Bill was approved by Congress in February of 1917.[1] Funding for teacher training and teacher salaries were provided in the three designated areas, agriculture, trade education and home economics. Monies were dispensed to states on a matching fund basis and the state departments of education scrambled to erect structures and set up programs. The home economics lobby and trade education advocates continued to campaign for programs in their respective areas and vocational educators reconsidered the exclusion of commercial education.

Home Economics

Fueled by interest groups outside the narrow circles of education, the campaign to promote home economics was particularly intense in the years immediately following the passage of Smith-Hughes. The AHEA (American Home Economics Association) was particularly instrumental in solidifying home economics' place in the curriculum. Public school curriculum and the education of future homemakers had been an interest of the AHEA beginning with the first Lake Placid Conference in 1899.[2] For reasons that are not entirely clear, they were not particularly helpful in changing the original Smith-Hughes legislation. Their legislative representative reasoned that home economics was being provided for already and they did not need funds. This position changed in the years following the passage of the legislation and the interest in curriculum and programs became a serious cause. Working collaboratively with the NEA (National Education Association) and the NSPIE (National Society for the Promotion of Industrial Education), the AHEA lobbied for expanded home economics programs to service students of various ages and life circumstances. The home economics movement successfully appealed to administrators who readily incorporated it into their programs. Home economics became a standard junior high school requirement in two-thirds of all large city schools, and departments were established in most public high schools and many collegiate institutions by 1930.[3] The number and percentage of institutions offering home economics courses grew from 3,161 or 26 per cent in 1915 to 8,072 or 44 per cent in 1927–28, and the home economics lobby can take credit for much of the increase.[4]

Armed with the Smith-Hughes legislation and the cooperation of the NEA, the AHEA set out to ensure that no young woman would advance through the public education system without proper schooling in homemaking, and they attacked their mission with zeal. The campaign to extend home economics to school systems around the country involved three main tactics. One was the employment of a continually expanding army of home economics supervisors at the national, state, and local level. The second was the generation and dissemination of volumes of prescriptive literature and course material for prospective teachers and departments. The third was the launching of a major campaign to increase federal funding.

One important medium for selling home economics to state and local school systems was periodical literature. In a continuous stream of articles that appeared in the *Journal of Home Economics, Vocational Education Magazine,* and the *Vocational Summary,* home economics educators argued for more classes, more perfect curriculum, more supervisors, and more home economics in general. Women waged an informal advertising campaign, using their print space to create an image of success. For example, one unofficial publicist wrote in *Vocational Summary* that,

> Vocational home economics is having a rapid development under the new system. Last year there were only five centers of vocational home-making. This year 21 high schools offered two-year courses devoting a half day to vocational home economics and related science.[5]

This booster club tone infused home economics educators' writings including those published by the FBVE (Federal Board for Vocational Education). The effect was the image of a highly successful campaign – a band wagon that everyone should join.

Periodicals such as *Vocational Summary,* which regularly reported on state and local projects, events, and conferences, also provide a good view of the administrative and supervisory network of women that emerged to usher home economics into state and local school systems. If, as Robert Wiebe suggested, Progressivism was 'The ambition of the new middle class to fulfill its destiny through bureaucratic means', then the home economists were quintessentially progressive.[6] They understood the importance of continual visibility for their work through publications, and the importance of an expanding cadre of supervisors at all levels of the system. They erected a home economics bureaucracy that served their cause well.

Home economics supporters had understood the importance of funding for administrative support before the development of Smith-Hughes. There were already two full-time home economics specialists on the Bureau of Education staff in 1915 and six women listed as state administrators in 1916–1917. However, the Smith-Hughes legislation precipitated a major drive to increase the number of federally supported administrators. According to the 1918 Annual Report of the FBVE there were supervisors of home economics work in thirty-one states whose main responsibility was to organize pre-service and in-service teacher training programs.[7] By 1927 there were fifty-eight full and part-time administrators responsible for home economics administration in forty-six states along with a staff of four federal agents working under the direction of the Chief Federal Agent, Adelaide S. Baylor.[8] Erecting a permanent bureaucratic structure was a highly successful strategy; the structure far outlived the fervor of the original campaign.

Federal and state agents became their own fields' publicists, writing scores of articles and bulletins, and arranging federal, state and local home economics conferences. Progress in home economics seemed to be measured by the production of these goods. For example the *1923 Year Book* of the FBVE reported that there were thirty-five state conferences and forty-seven district conferences held in 1923 with one state reporting that 216 out of 256 teachers were in attendance, and that the number of publications distributed had increased.[9] With remarkable acumen, the home economics lobby discerned the essence of bureaucratic progress; multiple staff numbers and paper output.

The drive with which the home economics lobby approached the task of creating visibility, disseminating information and lobbying for more staff was equaled only by the determination and organization directed to increasing federal funds. As home economics supporters were quick to point out, funding for the subject was an 'eleventh hour decision,' in the Smith-Hughes deliberations.[10] Funding for teacher salaries fell far short of needs and was considerably less than monies available for trade, industrial and agricultural education. Advocates, under the direction of the AHEA leadership, launched an aggressive drive to increase federal funding. They also enlisted a growing feminist political network, the WJCC (Women's Joint Congressional Committee) with the help of Maud Wood Park, a prominent suffrage leader and first President of the League of Women Voters.[11] In 1921 Congressman Fess of Ohio, the Chairman of the House of Representatives Committee on Education, sponsored a bill that proposed to equalize appropriations for teacher salaries. An impressive list of organizations sponsored the legislative drive and testified before Congress, including the GFWC, the Vocational Section of the NEA, the National Society for Vocational Education, (formerly NSPIE), and the NFBPWC (National Federation of Business and Professional Women's Clubs).[12] As a supporter noted, it was the first time a Congressional Committee held open sessions for hearings on a bill drafted for the single purpose of promoting home economics education.[13]

Although the Fess Bill did not pass Congress, the home economics lobby was intrepid. They launched a second campaign for additional funding in 1928 and with the help of Senator George Reed, (D, New York) federal monies expended on 'vocational home economics', rose from $57,774 or 19 per cent of the monies expended on trade and industrial education to $1,130,398 or 60 per cent.[14] The home economics campaign was extraordinarily successful. Not only was funding substantially increased but the structure of courses and supervisors insured a permanent place for the subject in school programs. Their success was due to the strength of the network and their political clout as well as the timeliness of their cause. The AHEA had state level organizations that were able to work with the network of GFWC which had branches in every state in the union by 1911. Home economics advocates had been working with departments within the NEA for years; specifically the Department of Women's Organizations, established in 1908, and the Departments of Manual and Industrial Training.[15] They also scheduled national meetings to coincide with the NEA, such as the August 1915 joint meeting of NEA and the AHEA.[16] Through the GFWC they had substantial influence on the House Education Committee and moreover, with the growing momentum of the campaign, enlisted the support of an even larger network of women's organizations including the WJLC.

While a great deal of the success realized in the campaign to influence public school programs was due to the political acumen and the tenacity of the home economics lobby, it was also true that they had a receptive audience in public education. Administrators and school boards were swayed by compelling arguments: most young women would become homemakers, and homemaking was sufficiently complex to necessitate school training. Senator John Sharp Williams (R, Mississippi) reflected popular sentiments when he said:

> We believe that at a certain stage of progress the pathway for the education of men and women diverges, and that there are certain things which after that time women ought peculiarly to learn ... Home economics is preeminently a question for the consideration and education of women.[17]

He articulated a perspective held by a wide segment of American society and in particular the middle class women, legislators and educators who welcomed education for the home.

Trade Education

In contrast to home economics, trade education waged an uphill battle. Theoretically, trade education for women had the same potential for success enjoyed by home economics: although funding for young women's trade education came out of the same general fund as young men's did, there was adequate funding available. However, trade education for young women never generated the backing or enthusiasm that home economics did. In 1929, more than ten years after the legislation was passed there were twenty-three women running teacher training courses funded by Smith-Hughes, compared to 229 men, and 283 women teaching comparable courses in home economics. There were 426 women compared to 2,302 men teaching trade and industrial courses and there were 1,463 women teaching all day home economics.[18]

Staffing was a key point in the implementation process and the shortage of personnel who were interested in developing programs undoubtedly contributed to the arrested development of trade education for women. There was one federal agent in charge of trade and industrial work for women, Anna Laylor Burdick, in contrast to home economics which had two agents established even before Smith-Hughes was passed. Texas was the only state to put a woman in charge of women's industrial work.[19] The problem with putting men in charge of women's work, reported trade education advocates, was that the men were not interested in women's programs: 'Most directors have the boys' work fairly well lined up but they know practically nothing about the work for girls'.[20] Even though Burdick was committed to trade education for women she was understaffed and apparently unable to generate enthusiasm at the state level. As a representative of the Federal Board, Burdick could advise state boards in 'the matter of preparing for the education of this new industrial personnel by establishing trade and industrial classes for girls and women, but the State boards must take the initiative in organizing such instruction ...'[21]

Inertia in trade education was the main concern expressed at a 1919 conference on Vocational Training for Women in Industry sponsored by the Committee on Women in Industry of the National Society for Vocational Education, (formerly the NSPIE and the Sub-Committee on Industrial Education for Women).[22] The convening of this women's conference indicated that the trade education lobby was still active and functioning and that trade education for women had become segregated from that for men. Trade education was suffering from the 'stigma which social prejudice has placed upon industrial work for women', asserted the women. Thus 'states and local communities have not taken advantage of available resources ... [and] only the smallest beginnings have been made in the establishment of systematic vocational education for girls and women in industrial fields'.[23] The committee called for an organized response in some key areas: the establishment of day schools for young women, the appointment of regional and state administrators for trade and industrial education, teacher training programs that would attract good teachers, and support for part-time education programs.

Some progress was made in trade education following this conference, notably in the area of part-time education, but in general the trade education lobby never succeeded in overcoming the basic resistance and inertia that paralyzed the movement. In spite of the efforts of women such as Anna Laylor Burdick and Mary Van Kleeck who argued that women deserved the same opportunities for training as young men and that industrial education should not be confined to traditional pursuits of women, the vast majority of states never wrote Smith-Hughes programs directed at women's trade education. The few that did were not successful in expanding the definition of women's industrial work beyond the stereotypes.

There are a number of factors which contributed to the failure of trade education. One consideration was the size and makeup of the trade education lobby. The NSPIE and NWTUL supporters were a small group compared to the home economics lobby: the total membership of the NWTUL never approached the GFWC's one and a half million members.[24] Their diverse interests which included worker education, union organizing, protective legislation and suffrage taxed the resources of their staff and membership. Second, their expertise was in political action such as lobbying a particular piece of legislation. Although the league had friends in education, they were not part of the education establishment the way home economics advocates were. For example, NWTUL papers and proceedings reveal no ties with the NEA. The NSPIE trade education supporters were similarly limited in numbers and resources. The Sub-committee on Industrial Education for Women was an active organization, at least until 1921, however the committee did not increase substantially in size between 1913 and 1920. Moreover, with the passage of Smith-Hughes, home economics became an important issue in the organization's agenda for women and the influence of the trade education lobby was subsequently eroded over time. They had been more centrist in their views on home economics than the NWTUL, yet they had staunchly argued for training for wage work. With the change in funding and the creation of state programs, they shifted emphasis toward home economics.

Suffering from a limited number of supporters, trade education did not gain visibility and was not incorporated into state level bureaucracies as was home economics.

Another possible consideration was the funding provision in Smith-Hughes. The trade education lobby on the Commission proposed a general fund for young men and young women, a strategy that was supported by Nestor and Marshall because they reasoned that access to money would be guaranteed. It is possible that a separate budget funded at the same level might have encouraged states to propose programs and appoint personnel to supervisory positions for women.

There are larger issues in the dominance of home economics over trade education that have more to do with the context in which this was all happening. The 'ideology of motherhood' was an umbrella issue, of which the teaching of home economics in the schools was only a part. As Sheila Rothman notes in her book, *A Woman's Proper Place*, the coalition of women's clubs and settlement houses constituted a large and very powerful group of women and the rhetoric of the movement of educated motherhood enjoyed an almost univeral appeal.[25] The organizational structures that were brought to bear on any single legislative issue were appreciable. The domestic politics machine was set up to move the Houses of Congress, state legislatures, and local boards of education, and the trade education lobby was no match for either the political power or the ideological power of the domestic feminists.

Commercial Education

Commercial education was excluded from state aid in the Smith-Hughes legislation by mutual agreement between vocational educators and business educators. However, vocational educators revised their position on commercial education in the years following the passage of Smith-Hughes. When vocational education leaders realized that they had excluded themselves from the fastest growing field in secondary education, they recanted and began to lobby heavily for federal funding. The FBVE issued a bulletin in 1919 discussing the need to incorporate commercial education under the purview of the FBVE.[26] The National Society for Vocational Education, (formerly NSPIE), appointed F.G. Nichols, a business educator from Harvard, to an Executive Board position and the organization came out formally in favor of federal funding for commercial education.[27] The Department of Commercial Education in the *Vocational Summary*, the FBVE newsletter, supported funding and supervision for the field; and *Vocational Education Magazine* lobbied for the same thing.[28] Despite these intense efforts to incorporate commercial education under the rubric of vocational education, however, the field remained independent of federal funds and federal control up through 1963 due to lack of cooperation on the part of business educators.[29]

Notes

1   FBVE, (Federal Board for Vocational Education), (1917) *Annual Report, 1917* Washington, DC, GPO, p. 11.
2   Williamson, M. (1942) 'The Evolution of Homemaking Education, 1818–1919,'

Ph.D. dissertation, Stanford University, pp. 197–233; Craig, H.T. (1945) *The History of Home Economics*, New York, Practical Home Economics, pp. 13–21.

3 Dyer, A. (1928) *Administration of Home Economics in City Schools*, New York, Teachers College, Columbia University, p. 22; FBVE, (1932) *Sixteenth Annual Report, 1932*, Washington, DC, GPO, pp. 36–45; Branegan, G. (1929) *Home Economics Teacher Training Under Smith-Hughes Act 1917–1927*, New York, Teachers College, Columbia University, pp. 90–92.

4 FBVE (1930) *Vocational Education in Home Economics*, Washington, DC, GPO, June, p. 24; Branegan, G. *Home Economics Teacher Training*, p. 65. It should be noted that FBVE statistics on enrollments included students from all types of schools, specialized vocational as well as comprehensive general junior high schools, and high schools that applied for Smith-Hughes funding.

5 FBVE (1920) *Vocational Summary*, 3, May, p. 15.

6 Wiebe, R. (1967) *The Search for Order, 1877–1920*, New York, Hill & Wang, p. 166, cited by Tyack, D. (1976) 'Ways of Seeing: An Essay on the History of Compulsory,' *Harvard Educational Review*, 46, August, p. 375.

7 FBVE (1917) *Annual Report, 1917*, Washington, DC, GPO, p. 57.

8 FBVE (1930) *Vocational Education in Home Economics*, Washington, DC, GPO, p. 34, vii.

9 FBVE (1924) *Yearbook 1923*, Washington, DC, GPO, p. 298.

10 Snedden, D. (1920) *Vocational Education*, New York, MacMillan, p. 52.

11 FBVE (1920) 'Provisions for Training in Home Marketing,' *The Vocational Summary*, 3, October, p. 87

12 On the Women's Joint Congressional Committee see Lemons, J.S. (1975) *The Woman Citizen: Social Feminism in the 1920s*, Chicago, University of Illinois, p. 55; Maud Wood Park's testimony is found in US Congress, House of Representatives Committee on Education, *Hearings on H.R. 12078, Federal Aid to Home Economics*, 4 February 1921, pp. 24–25. *Congressional Committee Hearings*, 280, No. 9; see also Sicherman, B. and Green, C.B. *et al.* (Eds) (1980) *Notable American Women, The Modern Period*, Cambridge, Belknap Press of the Harvard University Press, pp. 519–522.

13 Branegan, G. (1929) *Home Economics Teacher Training*, New York, Teacher's College, Columbia, p. 37; See US Congress, House of Representatives Committee on Education, *Hearings on H.R. 12078*, pp. 1–50.

14 Senator George Reed speaking on Senate Resolution 3969, (HR 15211), 71st Congress, 2nd Session, 26 February 1931, *Congressional Record*, 6038; FBVE, (1930) *Bulletin No. 151*, Washington, DC, GPO, June, p. 4; FBVE, (1932) *Sixteenth Annual Report*, Washington, DC, GPO, p. 83.

15 The department was called the Educational Department of National Organizations of Women. See Wesley, E.B. (1957) *NEA: The First Hundred Years*, New York, Harper and Brothers p. 287.

16 (1915) 'News, Notes,' *Journal of Home Economics*, October, p. 451.

17 Senator Williams (D, MS) testifying on H.R. 7951, Smith-Lever Agricultural Extension Bill, 63d Congress, 2nd Session, January 1914, *Congressional Record Senate*, p. 1832.

18 FBVE (1930) *Fourteenth Annual Report*, Washington, DC, GPO, p. 86.

19 Burdick authored one major publication and several articles as Special Agent for Trade and Industrial Education for Women. See Burdick, A.T. (1920) 'Trade and Industrial Education for Girls and Women,' *Bulletin 58*, Washington, DC, GPO, October; for articles see FBVE (1918–1921) 'Trade and Industrial Education,' *Vocational Summary*, 1, 2, 3, 4.

20 (1920) 'Trade and Industrial Education,' *The Vocational Summary*, 3, May, p. 14.

21 Broadwell, G.L. (1924) 'The Functions of the Co-ordinator for Girls in Part-time Education,' Master's thesis, University of California, Berkeley, p. 46.

22 'Trade and Industrial Education,' *The Vocational Summary*, 3, November, p. 98.
23 (1919) 'Vocational Training for Women in Industry,' Report of the Committee on Women and Industry of the National Society for Vocational Education, Chicago, in Margaret Dreier Robins papers, microfilm edition of 'The Papers of the National Women's Trade Union League and Its Principal Leaders,' Schlesinger Library, Radcliffe College.
24 Mary Van Kleeck is described in *Notable American Women, The Modern Period*, as a social researcher and reformer. She was a strong supporter of sex equitable vocational training for young women. See Sicherman, B. and Green, C.H. *et al.* (Eds) (1980) *Notable American Women, The Modern Period*, Cambridge, Belknap Press, pp. 707–708.
25 Rothman, S. (1978) *Woman's Proper Place*, New York, Basic Books, Inc., p. 135.
26 FBVE (1919) *Commercial Education Organization and Administration*, Bulletin No. 34, Washington, DC, GPO, June, p. 54.
27 Nichols, F. (1919) 'Federal Aid for Commercial Educaton,' *Vocational Summary*, 1, No. 10, February, p. 9.
28 See *The Vocational Summary*, 1–4, May 1918–July 1921; *Vocational Education Magazine*, Department of Commercial Education, September 1922 through January 1925.
29 (1924) 'Is Something Wrong?' Department of Commercial Education, *Vocational Education Magazine*, December, p. 1107; House Resolution 1055 in *Congressional Record*, 14297, 6 August, 1963.

Part 2 Conclusions

If the political maneuverings to influence federal legislation and subsequent program implementation are to be viewed as a contest between the home economics and trade education factions, then home economics was the clear winner. Home economics advocates who based their support on a more traditional prescription for women's role in society won out over the trade education lobby who supported, in effect, a reconciliation of women's work life with their homemaking role. As Geraldine Clifford points out in her essay, 'Educating Women for Work', American society 'refused to confront the reality that women worked [outside the home]'.[1]

Beyond the dialogue and the content of the decisions made, it is significant that women's groups from outside education were primarily responsible for defining federal policy. Progressive-era schooling was not unique in the fact that lay women influenced curricula; in 1854 women petitioned the Boston School Committee to introduce sewing into all the grammar schools so that needy children would be taught to sew. However the scale of the decisions to be made were new, the implications lasting, and the process of decision making represented a significant statement about the progressive-era women's movement.

The role assumed by women in defining educational policy was the outgrowth of several decades of attempts to shape education policy and programs at all levels of schooling. Women had worked for access to decision making and the organizations they developed in the late ninteenth and early twentieth centuries advanced their political skills. They learned how to influence decisions at the local, state and national levels and they carefully maneuvered their way into the halls of public power. Ultimately they were the architects responsible for the structures of women's vocational training. Yet, policy and prescription do not stand alone. In education they are put to serious tests when students begin to interract with them.

Note

1 Clifford, G.J. 'Educating Women for Work,' in Kantor, H. and Tyack, D.B. (1982) *Work, Youth and Schooling, Historical Perspectives on Vocationalism in American Education*, Stanford, Stanford University Press, p. 245.

Part 3

Curricular Programs and Practice

Part 3 Introduction – Curricular Programs and Practice

The high school in *Middletown* boasted a vocational program for its young women that mirrored programs all over the United States; home economics, which sometimes included dressmaking and millinery, and commercial education were the mainstays.[1] Whereas economics, ideology, prejudice, and feminist politics held sway over decisions about the scope, sequence, and content of federally funded programs, another complex of factors influenced course enrollments and what was actually taught in classes.

Based on what domestic feminists perceived to be a mandate for educational change, the burgeoning home economics bureaucracy created a curriculum sufficiently differentiated to meet all students' future homemaking needs and immigrant families', black families', and Hispanic families' vocational needs. Differentiated curriculum was an unself-conscious policy that was designed to provide students with an education appropriate to their backgrounds and perceived life chances. It was explicitly reproductive of social class systems and economic relations. As revisionist historians have pointed out however, it was difficult to implement, and thus not really successful.[2] For some older female students, afternoon and evening courses were a good thing, for some young black women who were required to take home economics and in particular to study subjects such as laundering, they were a travesty. In general the home economics empire was not able to provide the course structures they envisioned, and they were never able to inspire the next generation of students to assume the mantle of municipal housekeeping.

A rapidly-expanding and ethnically-diverse student population looked to schools for the credentials or specific skills that would lead to better jobs than their parents had; parents wanted that for their children as well. This vision was shared by many working class parents who were willing to forgo the wages of a daughter while she pursued education for office work, teaching, or more rarely, dressmaking and millinery.

Young women went to school for vocational purposes; it literally paid off in the job market. Thus they voted with their feet about the value of the courses. The choices would seem to be uncomplicated; you could go to work in a factory, laundry, or in domestic service after you reached 14 years of age, or you could go on to school in hopes of getting a job that had higher status and possibly higher pay. Basic English speaking skills, reading, writing, simple arithmetical computation, and the ability to fit in and emulate the social codes of the workplace were fundamental skills. Yet decisions about education and vocation were not as uncomplicated and seamless as they might appear. Students' race, parents' occupation, ethnicity, geographic location, abilities interracted with gender constraints and job market possibilities to create individual meanings and a patchwork of different patterns. Many young black women, for example, sought training in dressmaking as an alternative to the less desirable domestic service in private homes, whereas young white Irish women by virtue of family backgrounds were drawn to domestic service in 'good homes'.

The process of decision making can be characterized as one of negotiation. Given society's love affair with motherhood, (however one construes that); the reality of women's lives that served as role models for the next generation; the constraints of a segmented labor market that was increasingly accommodating to women; family backgrounds that heavily influenced choices; and the advent of a popular feminine culture that grew up around the image of the working girl; young women accommodated, resisted, and negotiated their way through decisions about work and family.[3] What is surprising about the period is that most young women looked forward to work and many saw education as a means to that end.

There are two principal points that emerge in this section. First, there were distinct differences between what vocational educators and interest groups intended for young women in schools and what young women actually pursued. Vast numbers of students flocked to commercial education classes despite warnings from educators that they could not find jobs, and elective home economics classes were effectively boycotted. Economic opportunities, or the lack of them, as well as students' and parents' aspirations were more powerful determinants of vocational course enrollments than prescriptive advice from advocates. Second, educators and parents were not in accord about the purposes of secondary vocational education for young women. They apparently agreed that vocational education should be sex appropriate according to their contemporary definitions. But parents and students, many of whom were native-born of 'foreign parentage', wanted education for white collar work in the short run, and enhanced social and economic standing in the long run. Programs that proposed to educate their daughters for domestic service or blue collar work in factories were unacceptable.

Educators, on the other hand, were much more inclined to accept social and economic hierarchies as givens, and they proposed programs based on those assumptions. Working class children were to be educated for blue collar work, according to the prescriptions, because that was where they were most likely to end up. These differences in perspective were significant because they resulted in educators offering programs that young women and their parents were not interested in and would not support, on one hand, and slighting other programs that were potentially rewarding on the other hand.

Notes

1   Lynd, R. and H. (1956 reprint of 1929 edition) *Middletown*, New York, Harcourt, Brace and World Inc., p. 196.

2 Kantor, H. and Tyack, D.B. (1982) *Work, Youth, and Schooling, Historical Perspectives on Vocationalism in American Education*, Stanford, Stanford University Press.
3 Anyon, J. (1983) 'Intersections of Gender and Class: Accommodation and Resistance by Working-Class and Affluent Females to Contradictory Sex-Role Ideologies', in Walker, S. and Barton, L. (Eds) Gender, Class and Education, Lewes, The Falmer Press, pp. 19–38; Valli, L. (1983) 'Becoming Clerical Workers: The Relations Between Office Education and the Culture of Femininity', in *Ideology and Practice in Schooling*, Apple, M. and Weis, L., Philadelphia, Temple University Press.

8 Home Economics: A 'Definitely Womanly Curriculum'

Home economics is an excellent example of a vocational program that held little interest for many students and parents but was strongly supported by educators and interest groups. With the help of Smith-Hughes funding, home economics educators built an elaborate curriculum structure and lobbied successfully for supervisory positions in state departments of education and local school districts. They became another fresh story in the bureaucratic 'superstructure' that Robert and Helen Lynd described in *Middletown* that consisted of differentiated programs administered by specialists.[1] In spite of the funds and human energy expended, elective home economics courses attracted a limited number of students and enthused few parents. The more permanent legacy was the requisite home economics course taken as part of the junior high school or middle school curriculum.

Differentiated Curriculum

The practice of adapting vocational curriculum to the needs of students of different ages, intellectual capacities and vocational goals was an ideal that home economics educators aspired to.[2] When the Smith-Hughes legislation was passed by Congress, home economics educators enthusiastically attacked the task of designing programs to meet the needs of all women. The curriculum structure was erected and vocational educators praised the efforts. There were full-time, part-time, continuation, and evening courses in addition to special programs for blacks, Hispanics, rural women and school drop-outs. The results of these programs were mixed. Sometimes they served a population well, as was generally true with evening courses for women, and sometimes they resulted in discrimination as seemed to be the case with blacks. In general, however, the structure and the courses did not live up to the expectations of their designers.

Students in school systems that availed themselves of Smith-Hughes funding were likely to find three categories of coursework available to them. The first category was all-day schools where students could elect a four-year, full-time course. When these courses were funded by Smith-Hughes, it was mandated that home economics work occupy 50 per cent of the students' time.[3] Other students who did not want to pursue home economics full-time could elect a course that would occupy one to five periods per week. The second category established was part-time schools 'intended to reach girls and women, either in the wage-earning field or at home, who can not attend school five days of the week'. According to Smith-Hughes guidelines, part-time programs were of three varieties: (1) where all the class time was devoted to homemaking; (2) where 50 per cent or more, but not all the time, was devoted to homemaking; and (3) where continuation schools were 'to promote the civic and vocational intelligence' of young women who have left school. Continuation schools frequently included home economics in their curriculums in 'amounts that varied from one-fourth to one-third of the time'.

'The third type of vocational home economics school, known as the evening school, is designed to reach the homemaker and enable her to enlarge her efficiency in that vocation'.[4] The evening school, which was often held in the afternoon to accomodate the schedules of homemakers, generally consisted of short courses in food preparation, sewing and millinery.

Age, marital state, and status in school were not the only criteria for a differentiated curriculum: intellectual ability, ethnicity, urban-rural differences, and race were considerations as well. Home economics educators tended to agree that all young women needed 'a well rounded-out vocational training', and they occasionally cited research to back up the claim that middle class women had as much to profit from home economics as did working class children. For example, a 1919 FBVE (Federal Board for Vocational Education) bulletin on home economics stated that according to a recent investigation, 'the proportion of undernourished children in well-to-do families is appallingly large'.[5]

Despite the claim that all young women needed home economics, however, home economics educators also argued that some young women needed more exposure to home economics than others and that courses should be adapted to the needs of the students. David Snedden suggested in a 1928 *Journal of Home Economics* that 'girls of less than median intelligence will probably be rearing two thirds of the children of 1940–1970 and thus the bulk of 'all money put into home economics should be used to serve ... girls of this type'.[6] There is little evidence that Snedden's suggestion was acted on, however there is evidence that adaptations were made based on the perceived needs of different groups. Immigrants, blacks and rural women were among the young women singled out for special treatment that varied according to what educators in different geographical regions thought they needed. First and second generation immigrants were a significant target population: home economics would Americanize young immigrant women and they in turn would Americanize their families.[7] Henrietta Calvin, a USBE (United States Bureau of Education) Home Economics Educator, succinctly described the relationship between home economics and immigrant education in a 1917 USBE publication:

Coast cities with their large per cent of foreign-born, adult population, have peculiar burdens and responsibilities in transforming this great cosmopolitan group into an intelligent American citizenship. Such transformation can not be hastened unless the home life of the foreign workman [can] be touched by American ideas of good living, sanitary dwellings, liberal education opportunities, and social responsibilities. In the accomplishment of all these changes, there is no more potent means than a strongly organized, well-supported department of home economics.[8]

To what extent was rhetoric and informal policy translated into curriculum practice? Were young immigrant women and other ethnic groups tracked into home economics classes? Evidence is sketchy because data were not published on special home economics programs. Yet, anecdotal reports suggest that some programs were established for the specific benefit of ethnic groups and young women were recruited to fill these programs.[9] Maude Murchie, state supervisor of teacher training in California proudly reported in 1923 that Oakland had an enviable program for 'the foreign girls' in full-time home economics.[10] A Massachusetts supervisor of home economics reported in *The Vocational Summary* that home economics and English had been combined in one of their evening programs to produce a successful Americanization program.[11] These programs were designed to keep or attract young women to schools, and once there, to teach them English while instructing them in practical concerns such as personal hygiene, child care (to reduce infant mortality), and basic cooking on a budget.

Home economics for Americanization has been sharply criticized by latter day historians as social control at its most severe. It is evident from the rhetoric that young immigrant women who were not expected to distinguish themselves academically were expected to profit more from home economics than other students. At the same time, however, it is useful to acknowledge the utility of these classes. Language was and is a severe economic handicap for young immigrant women; classes in home economics for immigrants may well have served to teach English and explain customs in a relatively non-threatening environment using familiar tools. Moreover, as Seller points out in her history of immigrant women, home economics courses may have made school bearable for some young women whose English language skills made sitting through a more academic class tedious.[12]

Training young women for domestic service was an important dimension of differentiated programs for ethnic groups. Twenty-one young Spanish-speaking women were released from their employment as 'maids' for part-time instruction in housekeeping, cleaning, cooking, and food service serving in an Arizona program which was deemed highly successful in training for wage earning and homemaking.[13] Similarly, young Mexican women were trained for domestic service in Texas in one of the 'best examples of training that functioned in the lives of the workers' that Laura Murray, home economics supervisor, had ever seen.[14] Home economics programs designed to train young women for domestic service seemed to be more prevalent in the south and the south west but there were also examples from other areas. For example, young Hawaiian women in Oahu were recruited for Smith-Hughes classes in 'Household Service'.[15]

This special treatment accorded to young minority women meant that they were provided with watered-down academic work, and heavy doses of practical domestic science. Like Americanization programs, the incidence of these special programs for minority women is difficult to calculate, however a Master's thesis completed in 1933 at the University of Southern California reported that between 25 and 50 per cent of young Mexican-American women in San Fernando Valley high schools were enrolled in special classes that were light on academics and heavy on home economics in preparation for homemaking and household service.[16]

Two other groups who were accorded special consideration were black women and rural women. Much like some of their working class white sisters, young black women experienced some subtle and sometimes not so subtle pressure to consider domestic service as their future occupation. Mary Church Terrell of the National Association of Colored Women and other women associated with the club movement supported the teaching of domestic science. She wrote:

> ... it is the duty of every wage-earning colored woman to become throughly proficient in whatever work she engages, so that she may render the best service of which she is capable ... our clubs all over the country are being urged to establish schools of domestic science ...[17]

The question of home economics for young black women is complicated by the fact that blacks were classified as a separate group and provided with separate educational facilities by virtue of legalized racial segregation. Very few young black women attended high school in the Progressive Era. In the year before Smith-Hughes was passed, there were only 64 public high schools in the rural south where the bulk of the black population lived. By 1932, this had increased to more than 1,200, yet high school attendance for blacks was still considerably below that of whites. As was true for young white women, more black women went to secondary schools than their brothers.[18] *The 1926–28 Biennial Survey of Education* reported that 'among blacks there were 82,074 girls and 50,255 boys enrolled in all public high schools'.[19] The payoff of secondary school was great: many young women went into teaching with one or two years of high school education.[20] It was difficult to track students into home economics courses without adequate facilities and material resources. In 1923, six years after Smith-Hughes had been passed, only seventeen states reported having 'vocational classes in home economics for negroes', and fourteen reported teacher training facilities.[21] Several of the federally funded teacher training facilities and all day home economics programs were concentrated in southern states. Louisiana and Texas, for example, had eleven of the reported twenty-eight all day schools between them.[22] Alabama had an unusually large number of all day home economics programs for black girls: there were thirty-three all day schools; twenty-three for white students, enrolling 4 per cent of the female white population grades seven through twelve and ten for blacks, enrolling 19 per cent of the black females in grades seven through twelve.[23] These figures suggest that there was outright neglect of programs in general, although some states provided course work and programs.

In addition to a general lack of facilities for home economics, those provided in many communities were inadequate. A survey of Wilmington, Delaware schools found the 'colored schools' to have poor home economics facilities: 'One room in a poor basement is all the provisions made for teaching cooking to colored girls', and 'there is only one room in this building in which sewing is taught to grade, high school and normal school pupils'.[24] During the Progressive Era black women's clubs lobbied for improved home economics rooms and equipment for the junior and senior high schools, however they were not very successful.[25]

Potentially more significant than the discriminatory provision of facilities were curriculum requirements and standards. A 1931 Master's thesis from Peabody College in Nashville, Tennessee reported that in sixty-six schools surveyed in ten southern states, 85 per cent 'make home economics a required subject'.[26] For example, in Memphis, Tennessee, girls who attended Kortrecht High School (where conditions in the home economics rooms were reported to be deplorable), were required to take home economics whereas all courses for white girls at the high school level were elective.[27]

Blacks were more frequently required to take home economics than their white counterparts, and in some instances they were encouraged to take special courses to train them for domestic service. Home economics was required for blacks in Winston-Salem, North Carolina, and when 'the sewing classes were filled and cooking and laundry classes went begging ... The School Board decreed that every girl who failed to give the required amount of time to cooking, sewing and laundry would be dismissed'.[28] Laundry courses which led to hard menial labor were not sought after by young women who were sent to schools because parents wanted them to escape the drudgery of their own lives; none the less, some schools insisted that young black women take the courses, in view of their presumed future employment as domestic servants.[29]

In an unusual program involving local industry, the 1915 Roanaoke, Virginia Board of Education 'turned over to the Roanaoke Gas School 87 school children for instruction ...,' and the community was reported to be very pleased with the resultant 'increased efficiency and contentment of houseworkers'.[30] The Armstrong Manual Training School in the District of Columbia was noted for its home economics curriculum which prepared young women for home duties and 'the service'. Charleston, South Carolina was reported to have an excellent manual training school for 'colored girls' that provided training in cookery, sewing, and laundry work.[31]

This curricular differentiation did not end with high school home economics programs. According to Fritchner's doctoral research, it even extended to the land-grant schools chosen to train home economics teachers. These schools were 'to prepare blacks for their vocational stations as cooks, housekeepers, and servants, a purpose that was not evident in comparable home economics programs for young white women'.[32]

It is clear from reports and surveys of home economics that there were many schools in the south that attempted to track young black women into domestic service and menial labor through home economics requirements and differentiated curricula. Yet it should not be assumed that young black women were altogether victims of a racist system. There is evidence of both criticism and resistance. W.E.B. DuBois was an outspoken critic of the limited aims of industrial education for blacks and he clashed openly with Booker T. Washington. In an article about 'Education and Work' DuBois criticized the lauding of black women's success in the household arts, noting that it should be attributed to their perserverance and general perspective and not effective teaching.[33] Another publisher-critic of industrial education questioned the reasonableness of teaching women about laundering, something they had been making their living at for many years.[34]

More subtle forms of resistance were noted as well. Walter Hogan described blacks as 'indifferent' or even 'opposed' to industrial education. H.M. Long, writing about secondary education for blacks in North Carolina, observed that students do not 'emphasize the value of such subjects as agriculture, manual arts, and home economics'. He went on to say:

This may appear strange, but these students indicated that these subjects are designed, at least in part, for the purpose of keeping them in their present economic and social condition. A similar feeling seems to be prevalent also among many of the principals and teachers in secondary schools for Negroes.[35]

It seems fairly clear that some young black women were being trained for domestic service. This covert tracking took them out of academic classes and subjected them to a strong message about their economic place in society. While the opportunity to learn dressmaking or plain sewing might have been afforded by a home economics course, like other sex segregated vocational training, there was an inherent collusion with the labor market to keep young black women at the bottom. It is important to point out however, that the percentage of young black women attending day high schools who were enrolled in federally-aided, day, home economics courses was less than that of young white women after thirteen years of federal funding; 9 per cent of young black women as compared to 14.5 per cent of white women.[36] The significance of these statistics is not entirely clear. Not all high schools offered home economics; some programs were funded by the state rather than by the federal government. Some programs for domestic service could be classified as industrial education and many programs were at the junior high school level. None the less, federal enrollment statistics suggest that, despite the requirements in southern states, the majority of young black women in public high schools were not being successfully tracked into home economics classes.

Rural women were another group singled out for special attention. As indicated earlier, home economics educators and rural life supporters agreed that rural women were leaving the farm in greater numbers than young men, and that the structure of farm life depended on attracting young women to rural life. Theoretically, home economics was the key to keeping young women down on the farm and preparing them for a rich and happy life. Thus an important goal of the home economics campaign was to bring home economics into rural high schools, where approximately one-third of the nation's families sent their children and where the facilities available for home economics were inadequate at best. Rural equality of educational opportunity compared to urban was an important issue for rural educators and that applied to home economics. Home economics courses in rural schools tended to consist of basic sewing and cooking and that was not adequate for the rural woman's education. As a critic described it, 'Homemaking at present means for most of our girls in most of our schools mainly making garments out of cloth and pastries out of flour'.[37]

The reality of life on a farm argued for a different curriculum. A 1915 study of farm homes in Michigan 'showed that 80 per cent of the living expenditures, as distinct from the expenses associated with producing the principal product on the farm, were met by cash earnings of farm wives'.[38] Rural women were involved in raising poultry, bee keeping, fruit and vegetable gardening and many other jobs associated with the farm, and a course of study that took these into account would have made sense. Milica County Schools in Minnesota were exceptional. Their curriculum included agriculture, business forms and law, and farm accounts for all first year students in their county high school, in addition to teaching sewing and cooking to young women.[39]

While home economics educators may have been reluctant to include an agricultural emphasis in their course work, some agricultural educators actively discouraged young women from pursuing their farming interests. In an article entitled, 'Who Should Take Vocational Agricultural?', published in *Vocational Education* one critic argued that young women in agricultural courses – 6 per cent of students in day agricultural schools were young women – were taking up space and money that would be better used for young men and that young women really weren't interested in agriculture anyway.[40] The point is that rural women might have profited from a broader curriculum that was more congruent with their potential roles, but gender prescriptions and lack of resources limited the rural home economics curriculum to cooking and sewing. A second important point is that enrollments in home economics in rural schools approximated those of urban schools: a survey of rural schools in New York State found that 28.5 per cent of young women in fifty schools in communities with a population under 4,500 were enrolled in home economics.[41] This meant that most young women in rural schools were not taking home economics, and although it certainly may be argued that home economics was not offered as consistently in rural schools, the evidence suggests that young women wanted preparation for paid employment. Like their sisters in urban areas, 65 per cent were looking forward to a professional career in teaching, office work, or nursing.[42]

The critical question having to do with home economics and the process of differentiation is, how successful was it? Were special populations shunted off into home economics courses that led to domestic service and was curriculum shaped to suit the needs of individual populations? The answer to these is a qualified 'no'.

Full-time, day, high schools were not easily diverted from their general purpose. Graduation requirements dictated minimal standards and even students in the full-time, vocational, home-making programs were only allowed to take homemaking courses for one-half of their academic loads if they were funded by federal monies. Thus full-time classes in home economics were not popular with students. In California, for example, where Maude Murchie ambitiously promoted differentiated home economics and compulsory home economics requirements, 0.4 per cent of full-time day high school students in 1930 (639 young women) were enrolled in all day classes in home economics.[43]

These all day classes required a substantial time commitment: students had to elect the course for not less than a full year and devote one-half of all their course work to it. This was impractical from the stand point of young women who were going on to college, unless they were going into home economics teaching. Texas was another state that had a very ambitious home economics program; it boasted the third highest enrollment of full-time, home economics students in the United States – 15 per cent of their full-time, female, high school population – yet it is evident that the vast majority of young women were not choosing full-time home economics.[44] If tracking young women into full-time home economics for their potential role as domestics or housewives and mothers was the objective, it worked to a very limited extent in full time day high schools.

Clearly the goal of home economics administrators to provide differentiated curriculum to all students based on their vocational destiny, ethnicity, and other characteristics was not a success. There were instances, particularly involving immigrants and blacks, where young women were unduly encouraged or even compelled to take domestic science when other coursework might have served them better. But in general the evidence suggests that differentiated curriculum was an unrealized vision and that most students opted not to take home economics.

Curriculum Content

The content of curriculum was a significant topic for home economics educators because it was the medium for reforming society. Homemaking ideals were to be translated into concrete curricula for schools. Curriculum innovations were designed and promoted to reflect those ideals. These included; home projects, home management classes taught in simulated homes called cottages, child care and child development classes that sometimes involved the temporary adoption of children by classes or schools, and the integration of academic subjects with home economics. The four year domestic science course for Brookline High School in Brookline Massachusetts incorporated science into home economics to produce an exemplary integrated and academic course. First year topics are presented below to illustrate both the detail and breadth in a curriculum considered ideal by the USBE.

First Year-
Chemistry and the physics of heat-
1. Study of flames. 2. Thermometers. 3. Boiling point. 4. Freezing point. 5. Heat: Production, sources, nature, effects, transference, measure. 6. Water: distillation, solvent power, hard and soft water. 7. Hydrogen; synthesis of water. 8. Study of air and its principal gases. 9. Carbon dioxide. 10. The common chemical elements present in food compounds. 11. Synthesis, typical acid and base. 12. Acids, bases, and salts in connection with food work. 13. Some organic compounds, definition, sources, formation, and uses. 14. Five food essentials.
Food and Its Preparation
1. Study of kitchen equipment. 2. Carbohydrates. Sugar cookery. Starchy vegetables. Cooking of sauces, soups and purees. Batters and doughs. 3. Protein. Albuminoids, albumen of egg. Preparation of egg dishes; methods based on results of experiments. Myosin. Study of muscle. Cuts of meat. Principles of meat cookery. Preparation of meat dishes. Gelatinoids. Connective tissue, bones, etc. Gelatine dishes. Nitrogenous extractives. 4. Fats and oils. Salad dressings. Beef dripping. Frying Sauteing. Desserts and cream. 5. Mineral matters. Physiological value and sources of mineral matters in food.[45]

The Brookline domestic science syllabus also includes a list of study topics suggested for the economics class, and for English themes. Topics suggested for economics included: the consumption of wealth, food and its relation to labor power, the housing of the poor and its relation to good citizenship, and municipal sanitary regulations. Home economics teachers and administrators were encouraged to correlate mathematics, art, and science courses with home economics, and vocational education publications were replete with glowing examples of this modern approach. Plainfield High School in Plainfield, New Jersey offered a course in household mathematics wherein the students studied household budgeting, measurement as it applies to household furnishing, space heating, and the advantage of buying in quantity.[46] Young women at West Technical High School in Cleveland, Ohio studied household chemistry along with cooking: and students at Los Angeles High School studied chemistry for girls, a course that included; 'what we breathe, ... what we drink, ... food adulterants, (and) ... soaps and cleansing agents'.[47] The NEA's (National Education Association) Department of Science Instruction devoted an afternoon to topics such as 'Special Science for Girls in Rural Schools', 'Applied Science as the Basis of the Girl's Education' and 'General Science for the First Year of High School', in their 1915 annual meeting.[48]

The FBVE reported in a bulletin issued in 1930 that 'Related science is now a definite part of the all day vocational program in practically all of the States' and they subsequently issued a Bulletin entitled 'The Teaching of Science Related to the Home' to encourage the adoption of the process.[49] A superficial view of these publications would lead one to believe that the drive to adapt science courses to the needs of young women was successful and that indeed the general campaign to influence young women's general education was entirely successful, however, a more careful look at the evidence provides a different perspective.

The adoption of 'innovative' curriculum strategies such as cottages, home management courses, child development, home project methods, and feminized science courses was generally confined to vocational homemaking curricula in all day schools. These curricula were designed for young women who were 'vitally interested' in becoming 'intelligent and efficient' homemakers and they generally required two to four years of full-time work in which they had to devote 50 per cent of their time to home economics subjects.[50] In 1928 there were 48,881 female students enrolled in all day vocational home economics schools as compared to 1,179,035 female students who were enrolled in regular high schools. This means that approximately 4 per cent of young women enrolled in regular high schools were in all day federally-funded, home economics courses.[51] Furthermore, students in day high schools who took home economics courses were enrolled in general elective courses where the sheer limitation of time prevented elaborate course development.

A 1926 survey of the senior high curriculum by George Counts provides valuable information about home economics curricula. In his survey of home economics in fifteen cities around the country, Counts discovered that only 4.7 per cent of total class time was devoted to the subject and that 'the home economics program is composed almost exclusively of two subjects – cooking and sewing'. An average of 30.1 per cent of all home economics time was devoted to cooking and 55.2 per cent to sewing. Household chemistry was accorded 1.3 per cent of available home economics time; home nursing, 0.4; and millinery, 4.5 per cent. Counts noted that home management, which had 8.0 per cent of the total time devoted to it, was sometimes merged with cooking and that the actual percentage of total school time might be higher. However, it is unlikely that it was taught frequently enough to alter the basic statistics.[52] This fact was not lost on home economics educators who frequently complained that, 'homemaking programs in many instances are nothing more than cooking and sewing repeated, year after year, almost without change, to the same people'.[53] This criticism emerged when Ellen Richards proposed an alternative home economics curriculum which concentrated heavily on environmental sciences; the objection was repeated throughout the first thirty years of the century.[54]

It seems evident that home economics was essentially a failure in terms of its own curriculum goals. Ideal curriculum based on a progression of content such as Brookline High School's course was rare. Even more important, students were not attracted to day, high school courses. The Biennial Survey of Education for 1926–1928 reported that 16.5 per cent of the students in 14,725 public high schools were enrolled in home economics for 1927–1928; of these, approximately 18 per cent were required to take the course.[55] As Counts observed in his survey of high schools, 'The girls who were supposed to rejoice at the opportunity of being equipped for the responsibilities of the home and motherhood have been interested in other things'.[56]

Low enrollments disturbed home economics advocates who frequently commented on it in publications. A USBE survey of Winchester, Massachusetts schools reported that 'Winchester has a home economics curriculum and the girls are not attracted to it'.[57] Similarly the principal of Girls Commercial High School in Brooklyn, New York, observed:

We must acknowledge that our homemaking courses do not hold the girls in school; and that they are entirely extraneous to the commercial work and are only of mild interest to the girl who gets enough practical domestic science at home and knows that she will always buy her clothes ready-made.[58]

The majority of female students in day high schools were not electing home economics, and home economics educators wanted to know why. A Master's candidate at Iowa State reported in her 1932 thesis that her survey of 595 senior high school students revealed that students were not interested in the subject matter. They wanted to meet college entrance requirements; they felt that they could learn the same things at home; they needed to prepare for employment.[59] Another study reported by Annie Dyer of Teachers College Columbia University found similar reasons for young women avoiding home economics; scheduling difficulties, college entrance requirements to meet, and the work was already taken in junior high.[60] A survey of Memphis, Tennessee schools found that 'The majority of girls in the Vocational High School desire to major in some subjects which will enable them to earn a livelihood immediately upon leaving school; hence they flock into the commercial classes. This makes it impossible to elect anything but the briefest courses in home economics'.[61] Young women went to high school because they wanted to prepare for future employment and home economics did not prepare for desirable paid work.

Some school systems responded to the lack of interest or resistance by proposing compulsory home economics requirements. Counts found in his survey of fifteen high schools that 'those in charge of high schools are of the opinion that the great majority of girls sooner or later will feel the need for training ... and many will not enroll in the courses unless they are prescribed'.[62] Dyer's survey of 360 home economics specialists, supervisors and city administrators found that 18 per cent of the representative communities required a course in home economics and Maudie Murchie's survey of 355 high schools in California reported that 27.6 per cent required home economics for graduation.[63] In spite of efforts on the part of some home economics educators to make home economics compulsory at the senior high school level, it never became generally accepted practice. Since home economics was required in 85 per cent of all junior high schools, students could and did argue that they had already had a course. Parents looked on the high school as an investment; thus they did not pressure school districts to require home economics. Some may have even opposed a home economics requirement as in the Nebraska Supreme court case involving a sixth grader where the court ruled in favor of the plaintiff and her father, stating that she did not have to take home economics.[64]

As unsuccessful as home economics was in appealing to young women in public, day high schools, it was very successful in appealing to older women who could attend evening and part-time schools; enrollments in federally aided home economics courses in evening schools far exceeded enrollments in day classes. In 1929 for example, there were 41,088 students in all day classes as compared to 93,450 students in evening schools.[65]

Evening school classes held in the afternoon were successful for three possible reasons. The first is that the older students who were often homemakers probably appreciated the chance to get out and socialize. A short course in sewing or millinery was easily worked into the day's schedule because evening classes were often held in the afternoon. The second is that the evening classes, which consisted mainly of sewing, millinery and cooking, (in order of popularity), provided some women with resources they couldn't provide for themselves: sewing machines to make clothes for their families and hat frames and materials to make their own hats.[66] The third reason these classes were successful, as compared with day classes, is that they required a low expenditure of time and energy and were voluntary: women could come and go as they chose, and they only lasted a few weeks. Home economics in public, day high schools required a longer commitment than evening classes, and the time spent in home economics was time taken away from other academic or vocational classes, such as typing or stenography.

Conclusions

The relatively low enrollments in home economics in day high schools, which persisted over time, represent a significant statement about the meaning of high school to young women in the years 1900–1930. High school was an investment in time and money and for many students it was essentially vocational in purpose. Most young women in high school were there because they expected to use their education, either to get a job when they left school, or to enter college. For the majority of young women who went to high school, homemaking was something to be studied in junior high, or learned at home; it was not relevant to high school goals. This generalization applied to all women, including black women, immigrant women, and rural women who could afford high school educations.

Rhetoric about the importance of home economics to the salvation of American families continued throughout the decade of the twenties in spite of the obvious evidence that increased home economics had no bearing on the divorce rate and the stability of family life. High school administrators were receptive to home economics classes and departments, and some favored compulsory home economics, but they were generally unwilling to mandate home economics in high schools and enrollments remained low.

The ideal curriculum that would transform society and socialize future municipal housekeepers remained a vision. There were some exemplary home economics programs that combined child development and correlated science courses, and model homes and home projects, but the high school home economics curriculum remained generally inhospitable to change, focusing on plain sewing and cooking.

Successes scored by the home economics education movement include building a substantial federal and state bureaucracy, increasing federal funds, and ensuring home economics a place in the high school curriculum which has endured over time. Home economics may have been an appreciable addition to schools for adults who took evening school classes and the young women who wanted to escape from academic classes. Ultimately, however, the home economics education movement in the Progressive Era failed to achieve its stated goals and resulted in a remarkable expenditure of public funds.

What is difficult to assess is the influence of the myth of domesticity on young women's aspirations. Home economics in the curriculum reminded students of women's place in the economic and social order.

Notes

1 Lynd, R. and H. (1956, reprint of 1929 edition) *Middletown*, New York, Harcourt, Brace and World, Inc., p. 196.
2 Differentiated curriculum was an idea that was popularized during the Progressive Era. Simply stated it meant that schools were to develop multiple curricula options to meet the diverse needs of students. Intellectually gifted students, the hand minded, those who needed to work following graduation from eighth grade, and women were to enroll in programs tailored to their vocational destiny. D. Tyack described the Progressive Era view of an efficient school as one that would 'measure and account for every child, providing different opportunities depending on his or her needs'. See Tyack, D. (1974) *The One Best System*, Cambridge, Harvard University Press, pp. 190–191.
3 FBVE (Federal Board for Vocational Education) (1919) *Home Economics Education Organization and Administration*, Bulletin No. 28, Home Economics Series No. 2, February, Washington, DC, GPO, pp. 16–18.
4 Ibid.
5 FBVE (1919) *Survey of the Needs in the Field of Vocational Home Economics*, Bulletin No. 37, Home Economics Series No. 4, December, Washington, DC, GPO, p. 10.
6 Snedden, D. (1928) 'Where are We Going in Home Economics', *Journal of Home Economics*, September, p. 628.
7 Ellis, P.I. (1929) *Americanization Through Homemaking* Los Angeles, Wetzel Publishing Company, passim; (1918) *US Commissioner of Education Report*, Washington, DC, GPO, p. 33.
8 USBE (US Bureau of Education) (1917) *The Public School System of San Francisco California*, Bulletin No. 46, Washington, DC, GPO, p. 468. See also USBE

(US Bureau of Education) (1921) *Survey of Wilmington Delaware Schools*, Bulletin No. 2, Washington, DC, GPO, p. 121.

9   *Vocational Education Magazine*, edited by D. Snedden is a good source because home economics supervisors were recruited to write monthly reports about their programs. See Smith, W.C. and Springsteed, C.B. (1922) 'Homemaking Needs for the Foreign Born Based Upon Location and Nationality', *Vocational Education Magazine*, 1, No. 3, November, p. 203.

10   Murchie, M.I. (1923) 'The Foreign Girl and the Full-Time Home Economics Course in California', *Vocational Education Magazine*, 1, No. 10, May, pp. 760–761.

11   Ellis, M. (1922) 'The Spirit and Aims of the Part-Time School', *Vocational Education Magazine*, 1, No. 3, November, p. 206.

12   Seller, M. 'The Education of the Immigrant Woman, 1900–1935', in Kerber, L. and Mathews, J.D. (Eds) (1982) *Women's America, Refocusing the Past*, New York, Oxford University Press; Violas, P.C. (1978) *The Training of the Urban Working Class*, Chicago, Rand McNally, pp. 177–182.

13   (1920) 'Notes, Home Economics Education', *The Vocational Summary*, 3, No. 5, September, p. 75.

14   Murray, L. (1924) 'Training of Mexican Women in Household Service', *Vocational Education Magazine*, 2, No. 14, December, pp. 1120–1121; for suggested course content see Ellis, P.I. *Americanization Through Homemaking*, pp. 242–256.

15   FBVE (1930) *Vocational Education in Home Economics*, Bulletin 151, Home Economics Series No. 12, Washington, DC, GPO, p. 140.

16   Lyon, L.L. (1933) 'Investigation of the Program for the Adjustment of Mexican Girls to the High Schools of the San Fernando Valley', unpublished Master's thesis, University of Southern California, pp. 26–39.

17   Giddings, P. (1985) *When and Where I Enter, The Impact of Black Women on Race and Sex in America*, New York, Barton Books, p. 133.

18   Bond, H.M. (1966) *The Education of the Negro in the American Social Order*, New York, Octagon Books, pp. 122–150.

19   US Office of Education (1930) *The 1926–1928 Biennial Survey of Education*, Washington, DC, GPO, p. 2.

20   Trenholm, C. (1932) 'The Accreditation of the Negro High School', *Journal of Negro Education*, April, p. 36.

21   FBVE, *Yearbook, 1923*, pp. 331, 356.

22   FBVE, *Yearbook, 1923*, pp. 308, 331, 357.

23   Calculated using FBVE *Yearbook, 1923*, for statistics on enrollment, p. 331, 356; and USBE (1928) *Biennial Survey of Education, 1924–1926*, Washington, DC, GPO, pp. 1064, 1068–1069.

24   USBE *Survey of the Schools of Wilmington Delaware*, pp. 120, 121.

25   Carey, V. (1982) 'The Roles of Black Women in Education, 1865–1917'. Unpublished paper presented at the National Academy of Education, Workshop on Gender and Education, Stanford University, February, p. 22; Brady, M.D. (1985) 'Organizing Afro-American Girls Clubs in Kansas in the 1920s', Kansas State University, unpublished paper presented at the Western Association of Women Historians, Annual Meeting, Mills College, May.

26   Patton, R.A. (1931) 'A Survey of Home Economics in some Negro Schools', Master's thesis, George Peabody College for Teachers, August, pp. 27–57, 58.

27   USBE (1920) *Bulletin 1919, No. 50*, 'The Public School System of Memphis, Tennessee', Washington, DC, GPO, pp. 32–33.

28   Vaughn, K.B. (1916) 'Some Colored Schools of the South', November, p. 588.

29   Ninety per cent of laundry workers in Washington, DC, in 1922 were black women. See Haynes, E.R. (1922) 'Two Million Women at Work', *The Southern Workman*, 51, No. 2, February, in Lerner, G. (Ed.) (1973) *Black Women in White*

America, A Documentary History, New York, Vintage Books, p. 257; Jones, J. *Labor of Love, Labor of Sorrow*, pp. 154, 193, 222.

30 Vaughn, K.B. 'Some Colored Schools of the South', p. 589.

31 Leake, A. (1918) *The Vocational Education of Girls and Women*, New York, The Macmillan Company, p. 92; Vaughn, K.B. 'Some Colored Schools of the South', p. 590.

32 Fritschner, L.M. 'The Rise and Fall of Home Economics', pp. 67–68, 92–96; FBVE *Bulletin No. 151*, pp. 24, 68.

33 DuBois, W.E.B. (1932) 'Education and Work', *Journal of Negro Education*, April, p. 60.

34 Bullock, H.A. (1967) *History of Negro Education in the South, From 1619 to the Present*, Cambridge, Harvard University Press, p. 79.

35 Long, H.M. (1932) *Public Secondary Education for Negroes in North Carolina*, Teachers' College, Columbia University, Contribution to ed. no. 529, p. 109.

36 US Office of Education, (1930) *Biennial Survey of Education 1926–1928*, Bulletin 1930, No. 16, Washington, DC, GPO, pp. 990–992; FBVE *Bulletin No. 151*, pp. 24, 68.

37 Eaton, T.H. (1922) *Rural School Survey of New York State, Vocational Education*, Ithaca, p. 198.

38 Snyder, I.B. and M.F. 'A Survey of Farm Homes', *The Journal of Home Economics*, cited in Vanek, J.A. (1980) 'Work, Leisure, and Family Roles: Farm Household in the United States, 1920–1955'. *Journal of Family History*, 5, No. 4, Winter, p. 425.

39 Foght, H.W. (1915) *The Rural School System of Minnesota, A Study in School Efficiency*, USBE Bulletin 1915, No. 20, Whole No. 647 Washington, DC, GPO, p. 41.

40 Works, J.A. (1922) 'The Place and Importance of Short Courses in Agricultural Education', *Vocational Education Magazine*, 1, No. 1, September, p. 11.

41 Percentage and number of students enrolled in home economics, grades eight to twelve:

grade	%	no. of students
eight	8.24	71
nine	31.55	272
ten	28.65	247
eleven	18.56	160
twelve	11.60	100

Eaton, T. *Rural School Survey*, p. 200.

42 Eaton, T. *Rural School Survey*, p. 240.

43 FBVE, *Bulletin No. 151*, p. 124.

44 FBVE (1927) *Eleventh Annual Report, 1927*, Washington, DC, GPO, p. 33.

45 Andrews, B.R. (1914) *Education for the Home*, USBE Bulletin 1914, No. 37, Washington, DC, GPO, pp. 89–90.

46 Ball, K.F. (1916) 'Mathematics Applied to Household Arts', *Journal of Home Economics*, 3, No. 10, October, p. 521.

47 Short, R.L. (1914) 'The Progress of Industrial Education in Cleveland', NEA (National Education Association) *Journal of Addresses and Proceedings*, p. 462;

48 Jones, M.E. (1915) 'A Chemistry Course For Girls', *National Education Association Journal of Addresses and Proceedings*, p. 1019; Twist, B.O. (1915) 'Special Science for Girls in the Rural Schools'; Severe, H.W. (1915) 'Applied Science as the Basis of the Girl's Education', NEA *Journal of Addresses and Proceedings*, pp. 1015–1019, 1020–1021.

49 FBVE, *Bulletin No. 151*, p. 40; FBVE (1931) *The Teaching of Science Related to the Home*, Washington, DC, GPO, passim.

50 FBVE, *Home Economics Administration and Organization*, pp. 16–18.
51 USOE (US Office of Education) *Biennial Survey, 1926–28*, 'Table 11,' p. 989; FBVE (1928) *Twelfth Annual Report to Congress, 1928*, Washington, DC, GPO, p. 31.
52 Counts, G.S. (1926) *The Senior High School Curriculum*, Chicago, The University of Chicago, p. 104.
53 Johnson, M. (1922) 'The Development of Homemaking Courses in the Part-Time Schools', *Vocational Education Magazine*, November, p. 209.
54 Dyer, A. (1928) *Administration of Home Economics in City Schools*, New York, Teachers College Bureau of Publications, p. 22; Jones, E. (1928) 'Home Economics as a Factor in the Success of the Modern Home,' unpublished Master's thesis, Berkeley, University of California, p. 39; Indlekofer, J. (1916) 'Cultural Phases of Vocational Training', *Manual Training Magazine*, September, p. 5; Williamson, M. (1942) 'The Evolution of Homemaking Education, 1818–1919', unpublished Ph.D. dissertation Stanford University, p. 227.
55 USBE (1928) *Biennial Survey of Education 1926–1928*, Washington, DC, GPO, p. 967.
56 Counts, G.S. *The Senior High School Curriculum*, p. 103.
57 USBE (1920) *Survey of the Schools of Winchester, Massachusetts*, Washington, DC, GPO, pp. 110–111.
58 *(1921) Journal of Home Economics*, April, p. 149; see also Roman, F.W. (1915) *Trade and Technical Schools of the US and Germany*, New York, G.P. Putnam's Sons, p. 301.
59 Wiese, M.C. with Friant, R.J. (1931) 'Factors Which Influence Girls For or Against the Election of Home Economics in Santa Monica, California', unpublished Master's thesis, Iowa State College, in FBVE (1932) *Suggestions For Studies and Research in Home Economics Education*, Washington, DC, GPO, p. 71.
60 Dyer, A. *Administration of Home Economics in City Schools*, p. 34.
61 USBE (1920) *The Public School System of Memphis Tennessee*, Bulletin 1919, No. 50, Part 6, 'Industrial Arts, Home Economics, and Gardening', Washington, DC, GPO, p. 34.
62 Counts, G.S. *The Senior High School Curriculum*, p. 105.
63 Dyer, A. *Administration of Home Economics in City Schools*, p. 13; Whitcomb, E.S. 'Homemaking Education', USBE Bulletin 1931, (1932) *Biennial Survey of Education*, 1, Washington, DC, GPO, p. 244.
64 (1914) *The Northwestern Reporter, (1914)*, 144, 16 December 1913–6 February 1914, St. Paul, West Publishing Company, pp. 1039–1041; Porter, P. noted substantial resistance to Domestic Science in Australian schools during the same period, see Porter, P. (1982) 'The State, the Family and Education: Ideology, Reproduction and Resistance in Western Australia 1900–1929', Murdoch University, unpublished paper presented at the Annual Conference of the Australian Association for Research in Education, 10–14 November, Brisbane, passim.
65 FBVE *Bulletin, No. 151*, p. 24.
66 Van Kleeck, M. (1914) *Working Girls in Evening Schools*, New York, Survey Associates, pp. 26, 31.

9 'Hats, Hats, Pins, Pins': Trade Education and the Schools

Trade education for young women was a profound disappointment to the women of the NWTUL (National Women's Trade Union League) and the NSPIE (National Society for the Promotion of Industrial Education). Trade education did not succeed in attracting students the way commercial education did, and it did not engage the attention of administrators and vocational educators the way home economics did. Moreover, it was never adopted into the curricula of comprehensive secondary schools, as both home economics and commercial education were.

And yet, theoretically, trade education seemed to hold great promise for young women. The dropout rate for young women was high: 50 per cent of all students left school before age fifteen according to Thorndike's 1906 study.[1] Even though the retention rate for young women in high schools surpassed that of young men, more than half of all girls dropped out before age sixteen. A 1915 study of students in Hammond, Indiana schools produced similar statistics: 60 per cent of the girls dropped out of school by age fifteen.[2] Those who left before they entered high school were likely to end up as unskilled labor, either in domestic service or manufacturing. A study of 'The Working Children of Philadelphia', conducted in 1921 confirmed the fears of progressive-era feminists and reformers: of the 3,312 children surveyed, two-thirds were young women, most of whom were in manufacturing and mechanical pursuits. Moreover, in 1920, 25.8 per cent of the female non-agricultural work force was in manufacturing and mechanical industries, exceeded only by domestic and personal service at 29.04 per cent.[3] Students and parents had good reason to support and participate in trade training programs and administrators who might have increased high school enrollments had incentives as well. However, both the number of programs offered and student enrollments remained low.

The failure of trade education is the primary focus of this chapter, and there are three issues of particular significance treated herein. The first is the influence of progressive-era attitudes towards women's work in industry on the content of trade education programs, the courses which were offered were basically restricted to feminine industries. The second issue has to do with the economics of trade training: did courses in the needle trades lead to better jobs and advancement? The third issue is the response of parents to trade education and what that suggested about their expectations of schooling.

The Evidence of Failure

Trade education's failure is conspicuously evident in enrollment statistics for high schools. There were 9,575 female students enrolled in all day trade education programs and courses in 1930 which amounted to less than 1 per cent of all female public high school students. The total enrollment for female students in evening, part-time, and all day trade and industrial courses, exclusive of continuation, was 28,089 which was less than 2 per cent of the total enrollment of young women in high school.[4] These figures stand in sharp contrast to commercial education which enrolled 286,984 female students in 1924 and was described in the *1929 Federal Board for Vocational Education Report* as a subject which enrolled 'more pupils than all other types of vocational preparatory courses combined'.[5] Trade education did not attract students and a major problem in attracting students was the curriculum.

Trade Education Curriculum

Trade training curricula in both trade schools and regular high schools resembled home economics. Sewing and cooking, which often included dressmaking and millinery were the essential ingredients in both home economics courses and trade training courses. Moreover, the designations, industrial education, trade education, and vocational home economics frequently referred to courses and programs that were the same. For example, the stated purpose of The High School of Practical Arts in Boston was 'to prepare pupils in the subjects that underlie the practical arts of the household and to provide definite industrial training for those who wish to enter some skilled trade'. The courses offered by this school were: household science, millinery, dressmaking, sewing, and cooking.[6]

The overlap between homemaking skills and trade skills resulted from conflicting expectations. As discussed in Chapter 5, many people, including an influential group of women in the NSPIE, believed that trade training for women should concentrate on, 'those industries which are most closely allied to the home'.[7] Studies conducted in Massachusetts on trade school programs for girls similarly concluded that the most desirable trades for young women to consider were dressmaking and millinery, both in terms of 'opportunities for advancement and the reflex influence upon the worker in preparing for right living and spending'.[8] Machine operating was a third choice in the Massachusetts recommendations, along with a one- or two-year course in plain sewing.

Many trade education advocates subscribed to the concept of dual roles, that is training women in income producing trades that would apply to homemaking as well. The effectiveness of the principle in influencing trade education is evident in the predominance of dressmaking, millinery, and power sewing in programs for young women. These subjects constituted the core program in all but one of the six day trade and vocational schools for young women in New York City, and they dominated the trade curricula of such well known schools as the Boston, Worcester, Philadelphia, and Minnesota trade and vocational schools for girls.[9] The ideal trade school for girls, according to a contributor to *Vocational Education Magazine*, was established in a converted apartment house in Boston in

1923. This school featured a curriculum that taught homemaking skills, 'keeping the ideals of home always before the students', and, at the same time, taught millinery, advanced dressmaking, and tailoring.[10]

The problem with curricula that concentrated on 'traditional female activities' was two-fold. As one female vocational educator expressed it, the problem is that young women are being trained for some vocations when industry is asking for others.[11] Millinery and dressmaking were the two subjects offered most consistently in trade schools, and dressmaking was the most popular subject. In the Boston, Worcester and Cambridge trade schools for girls, 'almost three-fourths of the girls enrolled ... in 1915 were registered in the dressmaking course'.[12]

And yet the number of women workers employed in dressmaking and millinery, (not in factories), declined remarkably between 1910 and 1940. Together the fields employed 459,640 women in 1910, 239,828 in 1920 and 189,649 in 1940.[13] Milliners and dressmakers comprised 0.028 per cent of working women in 1920 and this dropped to 0.015 per cent in 1940.[14] In short, the millinery and dressmaking curricula were inappropriate for the labor market. The number of available positions for the labor market was limited when trade schools for young women emerged and it diminished markedly over time. Moreover, with the advent of compulsory education and the reduced market, competition for jobs became stiffer; the median age of dressmakers rose and the period of apprenticeship lengthened. As one researcher noted, 88.2 per cent of all dressmakers were over 21 years in 1910 and the tendency has been to 'abandon the employment of girls under 16 years'.[15]

The second major point concerns power sewing on straw and power sewing on cloth. Of the three subjects offered most often in trade schools, power sewing was the least popular, and yet the garment trades employed substantial numbers of women.[16] In 1913 Maryland, for example, there were 30,921 women employed in manufacturing and industry, of whom 14,867, or 48 per cent were employed in clothing and cap and straw hat trades.[17] Studies on the monetary returns of trade training conducted at the time indicate that trade school training in machine sewing for factory work was not a good investment: young workers profited marginally from a year's investment in trade school.[18] Researchers from the WEIU (Women's Educational and Industrial Union) in Boston found that, 'the year spent in the trade school ... cannot be translated into terms of money as a year's advantage over the come up through the trade'.[19] A recent study of progressive-era wage returns, comparing the benefits of trade school training and on-the-job training found that young women trained for power sewing in trade schools earned only thirty-two cents more per week than industry trained women at the end of the first year and this doesn't account for wages lost in the year's training.[20]

Young women who wanted to take up power sewing found that they could get a job doing unskilled work in clothing factories and learn power sewing on the job. It was common for young women to find a job through a friend who would 'start the girl on the work, sitting beside her'.[21] On-the-job training was the normative approach to learning power sewing and from the perspective of potential trade school students, who boycotted formal classes in power sewing, it was the most cost effective way. Families who sent their daughters to work in industrial settings, believed that 'investment in a daughter's education beyond minimal reading and writing skills was unnecessary', as Miriam Cohen's research on Italian-American women in New York City discovered.[22]

Manhattan Trade School for Girls: Case Study in Success?

Trade school education was a failure based on the enrollments cited earlier, and curriculum was a major contributing factor. Some trade schools, however, were considered highly successful, if not ideal, by contemporaries of the period: The Manhattan Trade School for Girls was one such school.

The Manhattan Trade School for Girls was established in 1902 as a private enterprise and adopted by the New York City Schools in 1910. It was one of the most successful trade schools for girls in the United States according to accounts of the period. The curriculum of this school, which '. . . attracted world wide notice', was typical of trade schools established for girls in this period.[23] Needle trades which included dressmaking, children's clothing, lingerie, lamp shades, and millinery were taught along with pasting trades and power machine operations, which included glove and straw hat making.[24] By 1923, manicuring and shampooing were added to the course of study and other schools in the United States followed suit.[25] These feminine industries were taught in one and two year courses that ran thirty hours a week for forty-three weeks.

The school's emphasis on feminine industries can be traced to the influence of Mary Schenck Woolman.[26] The school was established by Woolman, who was an expert in textiles, a faculty member at Teacher's College, Columbia, a founding member of the AHEA (American Home Economics Association), and an influential member of the Sub-committee on Industrial Education for Women in the NSPIE. Woolman believed that young women should have access to trade training and that they should be lifted out of dead end jobs with education that would allow them to climb the ladder of success in industry, much the same as young men. However, she limited the definition of acceptable trades to feminine industries such as dressmaking, millinery, power sewing and some pasting of paper boxes. Despite the presence of women on the faculty such as Leonora O'Reilly, who was an outspoken advocate of equity in trade training, this most successful school remained a prototypical female trade school adhering to the tradition established by Woolman.[27]

Who enrolled in the Manhattan Trade School for Girls? To the extent that the school was successful in attracting young women, many of the students were first and second generation immigrants. Young Italian women, for example, were attracted to and did well in trade schools because they wanted to learn skills they would use in homemaking – sewing and dressmaking – and because needle-work was acceptable in their sub-culture.[28] Dressmaking was a desirable occupation for Italian women, many of whom had worked in dressmaking in their native country, and it was believed to be superior to factory work. Thus for example, during a seven month period in 1914, 'Italians made up 27 per cent, or 142, of the 532 pupils admitted', to the Manhattan Trade School for Girls where 70 per cent of the girls took up dressmaking.[29] Research on The Boston Trade School for Girls found a similar circumstance although they didn't specify Italians; 62.6 per cent of the young women trained to be dressmakers were either native white of foreign born parents or foreign born.[30]

The Manhattan Trade School for Girls served a very specific population that was interested in the 'feminine industries', and thus the school could be considered successful in that specific sense. Enrollment statistics which were often used to demonstrate the success of the school were deceptive. Many young women who were admitted and enrolled stayed for a very short time. As one vocational educator expressed it: 'Like all trade schools that have yet been established, Manhattan finds the question of withdrawals a very serious one'.[31] In 1914–1915, for example, there were 1,196 students admitted; the average attendance for the year, however, including evening school, was 610.[32] An Industrial Education Survey conducted by the city of New York in 1916 found that 'about a third of those who register in the school remain to the end of the course'. The survey went on to say that 'many of the girls who enter the school do so to get a start in some factory, and leave as soon as there is an opening'.[33] Thus, while some young women were enrolled to learn a trade, they were in the minority. Most young women did not complete the course and many used the school as a springboard into the job market.

In the preceding paragraphs it has been argued that trade schools for girls were not generally successful. They attracted remarkably few working class girls; their curricula based on the needle trades was out of step with the changing labor market; and they were not effective in preparing students to advance up the salary ladder any faster than their sisters trained on the job. Another fundamental problem with trade school education for young women was general ambivalence about women doing masculine blue collar work. Acceptable blue collar work for women consisted of domestic service, waitressing, laundering, and factory work that was repetitive, low-skilled, and generally did not involve heavy lifting. Vocational educators, including many of the prominent women who served on the NSPIE's special committee on women in industry, argued with conviction that young women deserved trade training, but they were less assertive when it came to expanding the definition of appropriate subjects beyond traditional women's work.[34] There were, however, two important historical events that promised to expand trade education beyond the narrow categories of the needle trades, World War I and the Smith-Hughes Act.

The Potential Influence of World War I and Smith-Hughes

America's physical involvement in World War I was brief: it lasted from April 1917 to November 1918. However, the creation of a war-time industrial machine to produce weapons, ammunition, foodstuffs, uniforms, and transportation for the military resulted in substantial changes in industrial life. The major change that affected women was the restructuring of their labor market generally, and their role in manufacturing specifically. There was no great influx of women into the labor market; however, white women took over jobs in manufacturing that had been reserved by and for men, and black women moved out of domestic service to take over the unskilled jobs in factories that white women had held. According to a recent study of the impact of World War I on women, 'The meteoric growth in the production of airplanes, firearms, and ammunitions drew thousands of women from their time-honored employment in domestic service, textile mills, and clothing shops into the iron and steel, metal, glass, lumber, chemical and leather factories'. Moreover, women comprised 20 per cent or more of the workers manufacturing electrical machinery, airplanes, seaplanes, optical goods, motion pictures and photographic equipment, musical instruments, leather and rubber goods, dental supplies, food, paper and paper goods, and printed materials. Writing in *The Vocational Summary* one observer of wartime industries wrote, 'The question is not what can women do, but rather what are they willing to undertake'.[35]

The entrance of women into new positions in industry during the short war raised the question of appropriate training. As a result training schools for women workers were established, and the future of trade education for women seemed a little rosier. Many of these training classes were conducted in factories as vestibule training centers. For example, Bethlehem Steel Company operated a school for women workers where the women were taught to use drill presses, gunboring lathes, turret lathes, planers, shapers, milling machines and to do bench work.[36] The Westinghouse Electric and Manufacturing Company held courses for women in drafting, and the Packard (Car) Company trained women to use lathes, milling machines, and oxyacetylene welding equipment.[37] In addition to factory training there were some instances of public trade schools expanding their curricula to meet war-time needs. The Boston Trade School for Girls taught machine adjustment and repairs for women in power-machine operating, and the Girls Vocational School of Newark, New Jersey conducted a class in drafting and machine-shop work.[38]

These additions to public trade school curricula served as demonstrations of the feasibility of expanding trade school curriculum beyond traditional definitions of women's work and as symbols of progress for women such as Anna Burdick, federal agent in charge of trade and industrial education. She wrote:

> It would be impossible to recount all the instances of all-day, part-time, and evening classes which indicate the possibilities of vocational education for girls and women in wage-earning employments ... they do indicate something of what is happening this wide country over.[39]

These were short-lived victories however. Prejudice against enlarging the scope of women's work, 'on the part of the employer and of men fellow-workers', led to a return to trade education 'as usual' after the war. As Robert Cooke observed in his 1932 dissertation on trade education for women: 'Although the World War temporarily forced an acceptance of the new situation, many of the prejudices have since been strongly reasserted'. Cooke's study revealed that the vast majority of trade schools for girls were offering millinery, dressmaking, and machine operating with very occasional exceptions in day school programs such as a printing course offered at David Hale Fanning School for Girls in Worcester, Massachusetts.[40]

The Smith-Hughes Act, providing federal aid for vocational education, was another potential source of change. However as indicated in Chapter 7, programs and courses were not developed, and staff was not hired to foster its development. There were few victories and limited change, but there is one area of success that deserves mention. Part-time classes attracted more students and provided more varied offerings than did regular full-time courses.

In 1920 there were 5,913 female students in all day vocational schools and programs and 6,859 in part-time trade preparatory classes. Women were reported enrolled in metal trades, electrical trades, chemical trades and printing and publishing.[41] Often these courses were initiated by industry such as the trade courses for garment workers in Los Angeles where the employers furnished machinery, the school and the teachers, or they were responses to local industries, such as in Massachusetts, where 'all centers of the shoe industry report numbers of women enrolled in part-time courses.'[42] These courses were significant for two reasons. First, they were examples of industry's willingness to support trade training for women under certain circumstances. Second, they indicated that some young women were interested in trade training that would advance their position in their jobs or lead them to new positions. None the less, it is clear that the number of young women enrolled in part-time trade and industrial courses was small compared to other fields such as commercial education.

Roots of Opposition

There were a number of powerful forces that worked against the establishment of trade education. One of the most important, as discussed earlier, was the deep-seated prejudice about industrial work and its effect on women and families. Industrial work would 'take them out of the home', weaken 'the taste and capacity for domestic management', and degrade them, critics argued.[43] Industrial shops were not regarded as desirable places for young women, and the negative sanctions imposed by society clearly affected the attractiveness of factory work to young women and their families.

Parental aspirations were a second major consideration. Many working class parents wanted their daughters to move up the social and economic ladder, and they believed that 'opportunities in the trades and in technical callings of civilized life are inferior to those to be had through high school and college education'.[44] Factory work did not improve one's lot in life. One illustration of this point comes from a 1922 *Vocational Education Magazine* survey in which one parent reported that they didn't want their girl to work in a factory because they wanted her to meet 'nice people'. Another parent reported in the same survey that they 'would not think of allowing their girl to work in a factory'.[45] In another example, researchers from the WEIU of Boston reported that the low enrollments in power machine operating courses were due to the fact that 'power machine operating leads to factory work which girls do not wish to enter'.[46]

Parents were also sensitive to the economics of trade school. Mary Schenck Woolman of The Manhattan Trade School for Girls found that parents felt they could not 'sacrifice' themselves further than the end of compulsory education and needed to send their children into wage-earning positions.[47] Whereas need prompted many families to withdraw their daughters from school and send them to work to contribute to the family economy, rather than sending them to trade school, other families chose not to send their daughters because they believed trade schools were a poor investment.[48] One vocational educator observed that, 'the average parent has yet to be convinced that education for the girl beyond fourteen, and sometimes even up to fourteen is not a waste of time as far as wage earning power is concerned'.[49] The Massachusetts Commission on Industrial Education, for example, reported that it was commonplace for parents to say,

'Yes, I could have sent my daughter to school a year or two longer, but what good would it do? She will not be any better able to earn'.[50]

Another major consideration in the failure of trade schools was opposition from male workers who feared encroachment from women. Male blue collar workers were opposed to trade education because they feared women coming into the trades and working for 'one-half to one-third less than the men'.[51] Unions were particularly adamant about training for women and the presence of women in industry and thus, for example, baking unions in San Francisco excluded women from the trade. When printing unions were questioned by Van Kleeck in her surveys for Russell Sage in New York she found that women '. . . would not be allowed to touch any processes in commercial hand binderies except those they are now doing and these are too limited to justify trade classes in public schools'.[52] Opposition to women in traditional male strongholds was particularly high following World War I. In Detroit for example, the Detroit United Railway shut women out of their closed shop. At a hearing on the issue a particularly passionate union spokesman 'condemned the employment of the women as "a fester and a disgrace upon the fair name of Detroit"'.[53] This opposition from unions and male employers was an important consideration in the failure of trade schools because without the cooperation of either unions or employers there was no market for women's skills, regardless of how well they were trained.

Conclusion

The NWTUL knew that in order to improve women's position in the labor market, they had to confront opposition from industry as well as barriers to nontraditional trade education, and they worked assiduously in both areas. They were not effective, however, in changing the parameters of women's vocational training. As an organization, trade education advocates were involved in suffrage, union organization, protective labor legislation for women, along with general organizational networking, and they were consequently spread too thinly to devote the necessary organizational resources to creating a visible presence in national, state and local education structures. Moreover, despite support from women such as Anna Burdick, the federal agent in charge of trades, and the Committee on Women in Industry for the NSVE (National Society for Vocational Education), the lobby for women's trade education was never large enough in numbers or resources to lobby effectively for the establishment of state and local trade education programs. The ideology of domesticity and gender constraints heavily influenced this dimension of vocational education.

While vocational educators pointed with pride to schools and programs such as the Manhattan Trade School for Girls and the Boston Trade School for Girls, trade education for young women in secondary schools was ultimately a failure. Moreover, trade education failed out of lack of support from the major parties involved in the process. State vocational education agencies and boards were noticeably inactive. There was only one state that established an agent in charge of trade training for young women, and there were relatively few programs.

The lone voices in the wilderness, the NWTUL and trade education advocates in the NSPIE were ineffective in promoting trade education among students, teachers and parents. Moreover, the NWTUL knew that in order to improve women's position in the labor market they had to overcome formidable opposition from industry and trade unions. They were not effective in changing the parameters of women's vocational training and creating a semblance of gender equity and over time shifted their focus on legislative means for changing work place conditions.

The bulk of evidence indicates that society, schools, and parents did not want to educate young women for blue collar work. From the parents perspective it was not cost effective, and it was contrary to working class family norms. As Leslie Woodcock Tentler's study pointed out, young working class women were sent into the workforce to support their families and to 'wait for marriage'. Education was secondary to family relationships and loyalties, and for some parents, excessive education was viewed as a detriment. It might make them unfit for marriage, reported some Polish, Italian, and Jewish parents.[54] When students did stay in school it was generally for clean, respectable employment such as teaching or clerical work which justified the sacrifice of wages.

Vocational educators and school administrators were influenced by the rhetoric generated about home economics and the ideology of domesticity. In the absence of any challenges from powerful interest groups, supported by a general societal belief that women belonged in the home, and considering the health and safety problems associated with the industrial workplace, there was no compelling argument for trade education for women.

What is very clear in the example of trade education for young working class women is that they were not compelled to pursue education for blue collar work, there was no coercion by virtue of required course work. But gender identity in the working class family, and an ideology based on women's social role in the family conspired to limit occupational choices.

Notes

1 US Department of the Interior: Bureau of Education. Thorndike, E.L. (1908) 'The Elimination of Pupils from School', Bulletin No. 4, Washington, DC, GPO, pp. 15, 28–29.
2 Leonard, R.J. (1915) *Some Facts Concerning the People, Industries and Schools of Hammond and a Suggested Program for Elementary, Industrial Prevocational and Vocational Education*, Hammond, Hammond Indiana Board of Education, pp. 65–66.
3 Ormsbee, H.G. (1927) *The Young Employed Girl*, New York, The Woman's Press, p. 41.
4 FBVE (Federal Board for Vocational Education) (1930) *14th Annual Report*, Washington, DC, US GPO (Government Printing Office), pp. 84–85; FBVE, (1930) *Vocational Education in Home Economics (1930)*, Bulletin No. 151, Home Economics Series No. 12, Washington, DC, GPO, p. 152; USOE (US Office of Education), (1930) *Biennial Survey of Education 1926–1928*, Bulletin No. 16 Washington, DC, GPO, p. 984.
5 FBVE (1929) *13th Annual Report*, Washington, DC, GPO, p. 51.
6 Leavitt, F.M. (1912) 'Vocational Education in the Boston Public Schools', *Vocational Education Magazine*, May, p. 322.
7 Hawkins, L.S., Prosser, C.A. and Wright, J.C. (1951) *Development of Vocational Education*, Chicago, American Technical Society, p. 34; Marshall, F. (1907)

'Industrial Training for Women', *National Society for the Promotion of Industrial Education Bulletin No. 4*, October.

8   Kingsbury, S. Department of Research of the WEIU (Women's Educational and Industrial Union) of Boston 'Industrial Opportunities for Women in Sommerville', p. 9, in the papers of the NYCBVI (New York City Bureau of Vocational Information), B-8, Box 7, Folder 59, Schlesinger Library, Radcliffe College. (investigation conducted around 1910)

9   For information on these early trade schools see, Proceedings of the NSPIE (National Society for the Promotion of Industrial Education), (1911) especially *Trade Education for Girls, Bulletin No. 13*, New York; Leake, A.H. (1918) *The Vocational Education of Girls and Women*, New York, The Macmillan Company; Cooke, R.L. (1932) 'Trade and Industrial Education for Girls and Women in California', Ph.D. dissertation, Berkeley, University of California Berkeley.

10 (1923) 'News and Notes', *Vocational Education Magazine*, September.

11 Von Baur, E. (1915–1916) in lecture 8 of a series on 'Women in Industry; Her Opportunities in Business Today', October 1915–May 1916 in the papers of the NYCBVI, B-3, Box 1, folder 11, lecture 8. Schlesinger Library, Radcliffe College.

12 Allinson, M. (1917) *Industrial Experience of Trade-School Girls in Massachusetts*, Boston, WEIU, p. 21.

13 Anderson, D. and Davidson, P.E. (1945 reprint 1978) *Recent Occupational Trends in American Labor, A Supplement to Occupations Trends in the United States*, Stanford, Stanford University Press, pp. 118, 122, 123; Hill, J.A. (1929) *Women in Gainful Occupations 1870–1920*, Census Monograph 9, Washington, DC, GPO, reprint Westport, Greenwood Press, p. 33.

14 Anderson, *Recent Occupational Trends in American Labor*, pp. 118, 122, 123; Hill, J. *Women in Gainful Occupations*, p. 33.

15 Allinson, *Industrial Experience of Trade-School Girls in Massachusetts*, pp. 9, 199.

16 Out of 2,500 students enrolled in the three trade schools for young women surveyed by the WEIU, 315 had taken courses in power sewing. The researchers commented that 'Power Machine operating leads to factory work which girls do not wish to enter'. Allinson, *Industrial Experience*, pp. 20–21.

17 Trax, L.C. (1913) 'Working Women In Maryland', *Life and Labor*, April, p. 100. Microfilm edition of the Papers of the NWTUL (National Women's Trade Union League) and Its Principal Leaders.

18 Hedges, A. was particularly interested in this problem. See Hedges, A.C. (1915) *Wage Worth of School Training, An Analytical Study of Six Hundred Women-Workers in Textile Factories*, New York, Teachers College, Columbia University, passim.

19 Allinson, *Industrial Experience of Trade School Girls in Massachusetts*, p. 146.

20 Aldrych, M. (1978) 'Vocational Education, Occupational Segregation and Women's Earning During the Progressive Era', unpublished paper Smith College, p. 7; Carter, S.B. and Prus, M. (1982) 'The Labor Market and the American High School Girl 1890–1928', *Journal of Economic History*, 42, No. 1, March, p. 163.

21 Hedges, A. *Wage Worth of School Training*, p. 8.

22 Cohen, M. (1977) 'Italian American Women in New York City, 1900–1950 Work and School', cited in Canto, M. and Laurie, B. *Class, Sex and the Woman Worker*, Westport, Greenwich Press, p. 132.

23 Allinson, *Industrial Training of Trade School Girls*, p. 6; Leake, (1924) *Vocational Education of Girls and Women*, p. 290; Reported enrollment for 1923 was 2,055 students in day trade classes and fully one-third more people applied for entrance on the first day of each semester than the school could accommodate. *Federal Board for Vocational Education, Yearbook 1923*, Washington, DC, GPO, p. 219.

24   On courses offered see (1918) *New York City Industrial Education Survey*, New York, City Board of Education, p. 100.

25   (1926) *Vocational Education News, Notes*, III, No. 7, January, p. 1. A publication of the University of California, Division of Vocational Education, and the State Board of Education.

26   On M.S. Woolman, see James, E.T., James, J.W. and Boyer, P.W. (Eds) (1971) *Notable American Women, A Biographical Dictionary*, Cambridge, Belknap Press, 3, p. 665; Woolman, M.S. (1910) *The Making of a Trade School*, Boston, Whitcomb and Barrows; and National Society for the Promotion of Industrial Education Bulletins, especially No. 24.

27   For information on O'Reilly see James, *et al., Notable American Women*, 2, p. 651; Lagemann, E.C. (1979) *A Generation of Women, Education in the Lives of Progressive Reformers*, Cambridge, Harvard University Press, pp. 88–113; L. O'Reilly papers in the Microfilm edition of the papers of the NWTUL and Its Principal Leaders.

28   Odencrantz, L.C. (1919) *Italian Women in Industry, A Study of Conditions in New York City*, New York, Russell Sage, p. 261; Ware, C.F. (1935) *Greenwich Village 1920–1930, A Comment on American Civilization in the Post War Years*, Boston, Houghton Mifflin, p. 341; Allinson, *Industrial Experience*, p. 7.

29   Odencrantz, L.C. *Italian Women in Industry*, p. 260.

30   Allinson, *Industrial Experience of Trade-School Girls in Massachusetts*, p. 177.

31   Leake, A. *Vocational Education of Girls and Women*, p. 290.

32   Leake, A. *Vocational Education of Girls and Women*, p. 290.

33   *New York City Industrial Education Survey*, p. 102.

34   The assumption that trade education would focus on the feminine industries is evident in most all of the articles published in NSPIE Bulletins on the topic, especially No. 4, 'Industrial Training for Women', October 1907; No. 10, 'Proceedings of Third Annual Meeting, Milwaukee, Wisconsin', March, 1910; No. 18 'Proceedings of Seventh Annual Meeting, Grand Rapids', March, 1914; No. 23, 'Evening Vocational Courses for Girls and Women', February, 1917. One of the few exceptions is found in Mrs R. Robins' article, (1910) 'Industrial Education for Women', NSPIE Bulletin No. 10, March, pp. 77–81.

35   Greenwald, M.W. (1977) 'Women, War and Work: The Impact of World War I on Women Workers in the United States', Ph.D. dissertation, Brown University, introduction.

36   FBVE (1918) *Vocational Summary*, 1, No. 3, July, p. 22.

37   Burdick, A.L. (1918) 'Training of Girls and Women for Emergency War Work', *The Vocational Summary*, 1, No. 4, August, p. 8.

38   Burdick, A.L. (1918) 'Training of Girls and Women', p. 9; see also Kelly, R.W. (1919) 'Training Industrial Workers', Ed.D thesis, Harvard University, May, p. 273; Moore, H.S. (1922) 'The Short Course as A Vestibule School for Employment', *Vocational Education Magazine*, September, p. 46, for discussion of vestibule training for women.

39   Burdick, A.L. (1918) 'Training of Girls and Women', p. 9; 'Women and War Work', *The Vocational Summary*, 1, No. 3, July, p. 22.

40   Cooke, R.L. (1932) 'Trade and Industrial Education for Girls and Women in California', Doctoral dissertation, Berkeley, University of California Berkeley, pp. 25, 71.

41   Ibid., pp. 64–80.

42   MacLear, M. (1923) 'Trade Education for Girls Under the Smith-Hughes Act', *Vocational Education Magazine*, December, p. 313; Burbank, E. (1923) 'Profitable Training for Girls', *Vocational Education Magazine*, April, p. 610; Patty, W.W. (1920) 'Opportunities for Vocational Education in California Evening High Schools', Master's thesis, Berkeley, University of Caifornia, Berkeley, p. 37;

(1919) 'Women Workers are Trained for Promotion', *Vocational Summary*, 2, No. 2, June, p. 34.

43 Henry, A. (1973) *The Trade Union Woman*, New York, Burt Franklin, p. 185. (reprint edition); Weatherly, U.G. (1909) 'How Does the Access of Women to Industrial Occupations React on the Family?' in *Papers and Proceedings of the American Sociological Society, Third Annual Meeting*, Chicago, University of Chicago Press, p. 124.

44 Snedden, D. (1923) 'The Carnegie Foundation Report', *Vocational Education Magazine*, 1, No. 8, April, p. 561.

45 Ells, M.C. (1922) 'The Spirit and Aims of Part-Time Schools', *Vocational Education Magazine*, November, p. 206.

46 Allinson, *Industrial Experience of Trade-School Girls in Massachusetts*, pp. 20–21.

47 Woolman, M.S. (1910) *The Making of a Trade School*, Boston, Whitcomb and Barrows, p. 9.

48 For discussion of family economy and working-class daughters see Tentler, L.W. (1979) *Wage Earning Women; Industrial Work and Family Life in the United States, 1900–1930*, New York, Oxford University Press, pp. 85–114; Tilly, L. and Scott, J. (1978) *Women, Work and Family*, New York, Holt, Rinehart, Winston, p. 177.

49 Leake, *Vocational Education of Girls and Women*, p. 261.

50 Marshall, F. (1907) 'Industrial Training for Women', NSPIE, *Bulletin No. 4*, p. 50.

51 McDowell, M. (1913) 'Women at Work', *Life and Labor*, July, p. 197.

52 Van Kleeck, *Women in the Bookbinding Trade*, p. 214.

53 Report of Hearing Before Examiners, 16 September 1918, Docket No. 265, National War Labor Board Records, Entry 10, Group I: Examiners' Reports, Street Railway Cases, cited by Conner, V.J. (1979/1980) '"The Mothers of the Race" in World War I: The National War Labor Board and Women in Industry', *Labor History*, 21, Winter, p. 31.

54 Tentler, L.W. (1979) *Wage Earning Women; Industrial Work and Family Life in the United States, 1900–1930*, New York, Oxford University Press, p. 100.

10   The Success of Commercial Education

Commercial education was the vocational success story of high schools in the Progressive Era. Students, parents, administrators, and eventually vocational educators supported commercial education and in contrast to home economics and trade education; course and program enrollments grew impressively between 1900 and 1930. The number of public high school students enrolled in business courses rose from 519,000 in 1900 to 4,497,000 in 1934 and the percentage enrolled jumped from 21.7 per cent in 1900 to 57.7 per cent in 1934.[1] These figures indicated the presence of an expanding army of office workers that was increasingly dominated by women. Young women who aspired to office work flocked to commercial courses in public high schools to learn typing, stenography, and bookkeeping, and the population of commercial education courses was steadily feminized. In 1914 56 per cent of students in commercial courses were young women, and by 1924 the percentage had risen to 67.[2] High schools accommodated these students by hiring more teachers, adding more classes, both day and evening, and in some cases building high schools to house commercial education.[3] Commercial education in high schools was thus a response to the growth and increasing feminization of office work.

The feminization of commercial education in secondary schools was a problem for people who envisioned high schools as training grounds for corporate captains rather than clerical workers. Yet allegations of feminization and loss of status could not change the course of progress. Programs continued to accommodate young women who looked for skills that were marketable in offices, and they remained inhospitable to the influence of visionaries who wanted them to become training programs for general business.

The following chapter focuses on the development of commercial education in secondary schools paying particular attention to expansion, feminization, and the response of students and vocational educators. The main argument of this chapter is that commerical education was a testimonial to the influence of students and parents in high school programs. Given the receptive labor market, young women wanted to be office workers and they turned to schools for training: first to private business schools and then to public schools as programs were developed and expanded. Public schools responded to the demands of young women, and to competition from private business schools which threatened to lure students, by adding courses and programs in typing, stenography, bookkeeping, and business arithmetic. Attempts to change the primary focus of commercial education from basic skill development for clerical work to management training were not successful and thus programs were not attractive to many young men. Moreover, attempts by vocational educators to incorporate commercial education under the umbrella of vocational education were not successful either, the field remained autonomous. Young women flocked to commercial classes because they provided skills that converted to jobs. They voted with their feet, and along with a receptive labor market, were responsible for the success of commercial education in secondary schools.

Growth and Expansion

Accounts of the growth of commercial courses serve both to remind us of their popular appeal and to document the amazement of school leaders over their success. As Janice Weiss noted, surveys of commerical education abounded, especially in the years after Smith-Hughes was passed, and predictably their results revealed growth and more growth. When the WEIU (Women's Educational and Industrial Union) investigated office work for girls in Boston in 1913, they found that nine of the eleven high schools in Boston offered commercial courses and 3,699 or 63.4 per cent of the girls enrolled in these schools were taking one or more commercial subjects.[4] The reported enrollment for commercial subjects in Girls High School, Philadelphia, ten years later, was 687 out of 1,162 girls or 59.1 per cent.[5] George Counts commented on the popularity of commercial education in his 1924 survey of fifteen senior high schools, noting that 'commercial subjects have come to occupy a place in the program of studies second only to English based on the amount of time devoted to the coursework'.[6] The appeal of commercial courses was equally evident in evening school work. In California evening schools, according to a survey conducted in 1919–1920, two of the three most popular courses both in terms of the number of schools offering and enrollments, were typing and shorthand.[7] These impressive enrollment figures were not surprising given the aspirations of young women for office work; in many places, the combination of stenography and typing which equipped young women to be private secretaries rivaled all other occupations by 1930 including teaching. Twenty years of vocational surveying in communities scattered around the United States documented the aspirations of young women. Surveys of eighth graders in San Francisco in 1916, eighth graders in Baltimore in 1922 and tenth graders in San Jose, California in 1931, listed office work as the top occupational choice, with teaching listed as the second most popular vocation.[8]

The Problem of Feminization

Commercial education was clearly a success story, however the enthusiasm of female students for commercial education programs was not always matched by the enthusiasm of school administrators, commercial educators, and vocational educators. Administrators were happy to have their high schools populated and expanding, and the vitality of commercial education served that purpose well. However administrators such as Frank Thompson of Boston and Alfred Roncovieri of San Francisco wanted to create a strong link between high schools and the exciting and powerful worlds of business and commerce.[9] Roncovieri, for example, argued that the San Francisco High School of Commerce should be training the youth of San Francisco for 'wider business occupations in the great mercantile world and not be limited to the narrower field of office employment'.[10] It was generally conceded that women did not have an important role to play in the the the world of finance and business, and moreover their strong presence in commercial education courses and programs was an irritant to men who wanted commercial education to become their link to corporate captains. Complaints about the 'feminization' of commercial courses and the inappropriateness of curriculum were common. 'Boys should not be preparing for clerical positions in competition with lower-paid women workers', argued Barnhart of the FBVE (Federal Board for Vocational Education) in 1923. 'When will our commercial schools awaken to the significance of the feminization of their courses and start to develop courses more suitable for boys? For business men rather than for clerks?', Barnhart asked the readers of *Vocational Education Magazine*.[11]

One suggestion for grappling with the problem of feminization was differentiated course work; for girls training for typing and stenography, and for boys a broader curriculum that would include studies of economic geography, law, and economics. The NEA (National Education Association) Commission on the Reorganization of Secondary Education outlined recommendations for commercial education in their 1919 report that included differentiated course work for: (1) stenographers, (2) bookkeepers and clerks for general office work, (3) secretarial work for young women who want to take more responsible positions, (4) separate training for young men and young women with an emphasis on a broad commercial education for young men and (5) training for salesmanship, [including] business principles, merchandising, and the cultivation of taste. The author of the NEA report went on to point out that, 'The conclusion sometimes made that commercial education should be for girls only is based on false premises. Commercial education should have a much wider purpose than the training of stenographers'.[12]

According to Janice Weiss, salesmanship was seized upon by men such as Frank Thompson of Boston who wanted to see curricula for young women and men differentiated and hoped that salesmanship would become a masculine domain.[13] Vocational educators were drawn to the subject as well because it held the promise of an entering wedge into commercial education, and moreover local merchants were interested in promoting it.[14] Macy's in New York, Filene's in Boston and the Emporium in San Francisco are examples of stores that instituted training programs in cooperation with the local school systems, however the programs fell far short of the lofty visions of men who aspired to training programs for business careers.[15]

J.O. Malott, Specialist in Commercial Education for the USBE (United States Bureau of Education), pointed out the lack of progress in critical areas of commercial education in the *1926–1928 Biennial Survey of Education*. Among the problems that he identified were tremendous increases in enrollments, 'particular-ly for women', 'failure to develop a continuous program of education for busi-ness', and a failure to promote retail selling.[16] Malott's perceptions were accurate; classes in salesmanship were adopted by some communities, however they tended to be part-time co-op courses, often held in the stores where young people worked, and they were identified with trade and industrial education, which provided their funding after 1917.[17]

Salesmanship failed to become the launching pad for businesss careers for a number of reasons. Commercial education teachers were not enamored with the idea of salesmanship training and did not support it. There was a shortage of teachers who were qualified to teach the subject because most commercial educa-tion teachers were trained to teach the traditional business education subjects of typing, shorthand, bookkeeping, and business machines.[18] Furthermore, the content of salesmanship curricula was vaguely defined despite attempts by va-rious agencies such as the FBVE to systematize it. Thus the classes failed to attract the anticipated swarms of young men.[19] The lack of interest was not due to rigorous job requirements. Sales clerking required a decent appearance, a fundamental ability to communicate [usually in English], basic mathematics, and the ability to fill out necessary sales forms and follow store procedures. Training on the job by store personnel was the most efficient means of socializing young sales clerks, which argued for part-time continuation or evening classes held in the stores, not full-time salesmanship courses in day schools.

The feminine underpinnings of salesmanship training was another factor which militated against the upgrading of curricula to training for the world of commerce. Lucinda Prince of Boston was credited with establishing and promot-ing the field of salesmanship along with the help of the WEIU of Boston and eventually Simmons College.[20] Saleswork, argued Prince and her contempor-aries, was a growing field of employment for women: in 1910, 28.8 per cent of sales clerks were women as compared to 41.2 per cent in 1920.[21] Butler wrote that 'no other occupation seems so desirable as "clerking" to the girl with some personal ambition but without the training necessary for an office position'. The field was accessible and for some seemed glamorous. Silent screen heroines such as Gloria Swanson and Mary Pickford romanticized the 'sexy sales lady' in film.[22] Also it put women in one of the fastest growing institutions in America, the department store. Thus, true of commercial education generally, women fur-nished an eager, competent and inexpensive work force that resulted in the feminization of the field.

Attempts to upgrade the status of commercial education by adding special course work and increasing the male population, were not successful nor were the bids for federal funding.[23] The business community was generally not in-terested; the business education community did not want to be associated with the vocational education movement because of its association with young people of presumed lower ability and social standing; 'and commercial educators saw their purpose in the high school primarily as preparing students for clerical work'.[24] Given a labor market demand for office workers well trained in typing, stenography, bookkeeping, and fundamental English skills, the core curriculum remained the same with large enrollments in those courses. The feminization of clerical work and programs that trained for it increased steadily, despite laments from business educators.[25]

Students

And who were the students who aspired to work in offices and therefore filled the commercial classes in high schools? Students in rural and urban communities and students representing various ethnic groups aspired to work in an office and filled typing, stenography and bookkeeping classes. As George Counts found in his survey of *The Senior High School Curriculum* in communities as diverse as Pueblo, New Mexico, Lincoln, Nebraska and Detroit, Michigan, commercial education was universally popular.[26] Women everywhere wanted to be office workers, and they showed up at urban and rural high schools asking for it.

The Fifteenth Annual Report of the Federal Board for Vocational Education stated that one or more commercial subjects were being taught in almost 75 per cent of the three-and four-year accredited high schools in South Dakota and that 205 of 301 high schools in communities of less than 5,000 population taught some commercial subjects. The same report noted that 37 per cent of all high school pupils in Montana were enrolled in commercial courses; 29 per cent in New Mexico, 48 per cent in Indiana, and 'nearly one-third' in Kansas. The author of this report was critical of the fact that commercial studies were not adapted to the needs of farm youth and suggested that farm bookkeeping and farm arithmetic should be substituted for the usual course outlines.[27] One rural educator commented that stenography was not a desirable occupation for the farmer's daughter to enter; however, there is little evidence to suggest that such advice was heeded.[28]

Commercial education drew students from different ethnic groups and social classes as well, even though opportunities for jobs were restricted for some young women. Many commercial education students were native born of foreign parentage as indicated in a 1914 study of commercial education. It reported that two-thirds of the young women taking classes in the evening commercial schools were of foreign parentage. Italian women, for example, who 'abandoned their prejudice against clerical work', and sent their daughters to work in offices, looked to the schools for training.[29] Young Latin-American women in Texas enrolled in commercial classes in hopes of finding a job even though employers generally, and some Latin-American employers specifically, restricted jobs to fair-skinned, English-speaking women.[30] Even a small percentage of determined young black women could be found studying typing and stenography although they encountered persistent exclusion from office work; less than 1 per cent of clerical workers in 1920 were black.[31] As the GFWC's *Bulletin* reported in one article, 'There is not a ghost of a chance for a colored girl to get a position as stenographer.'[32] Attempts to subvert student and parent goals did not work easily. As a GFWC member observed about young black women in commercial education, they might not have any chance of getting a job but these days it would not be a good idea to suggest that they take domestic science instead.[33]

Income was a fairly reliable predictor of who would enroll in commercial education classes. The 1914 study of office work conducted by the WEIU found that of 5,832 female students enrolled in nine Boston high schools an average of 63.4 per cent elected one or more 'technical commercial subjects'.

However in the poorer neighborhoods – described by the researcher as congested – 80 per cent of the students elected commercial subjects, as compared to 50 per cent in the more comfortable suburban neighborhoods.[34] Counts'

1919–1920 research on high schools corroborated this finding. In Bridgeport, Connecticut, 88 per cent of the daughters of 'common laborers' were enrolled in commercial courses, whereas 57 per cent of the daughters of professional men were in college preparatory courses.[35]

For young women such as those who lived in Bridgeport, Connecticut, clerical work represented economic and social mobility, and it seemed to be a vast improvement over factory work. 'He don't want the girls to go into no factory work if he can help it', stated a Middletown working class parent; office work was the answer.[36] Office work was cleaner than factory work, less physically exhausting, and generally better paying. The hours were consistently shorter, the work more varied, and it carried more status than either factory work or department store sales. It was, according to Professor Grace Coyle of Barnard College 'the most accessible rung by which many workers may climb "up" on the socially established ladder'.[37]

First generation Americans were among those who wanted their daughters to do better than they had done, and to meet eligible young men, and they were willing to endure sacrifices to make that possible. Schools were entries to the perceived benefits of American society: white collar work, higher status and greater material rewards.[38] As one Philadelphia parent expressed it, 'we do by our children in school what we can afford'. Commercial classes were afforded by many parents who could send their daughters to high school for one or two years, if they could not afford the three years necessary for a diploma. For young women commercial education represented an escape from the immediacy and oppression of poverty. Or as Ruth Coole found in her survey of young Latina girls, a vocation such as clerking held the promise of social position, 'so others will look up to me', and the 'chance to wear good clothes'.[39] For better or for worse, clerking took many young women out of working class ghettos, if only for the time they spent at work. In doing so it fueled ambitions and may have exacerbated tensions between parents and daughters. The following sympathetic view of young Jewish women explains the attraction of clerical work:

> At work a girl's in a light, attractive office among well-dressed people. She shares important business secrets. She hears and speaks English only. Her betters treat her with respect and speak to her like a countess. She's called 'Miss', and is asked how she feels and what she thinks. But at home, living in dirty rooms, she's plain 'Beyle' or 'Khontshe'. Her parents speak crudely to her. They pounce upon her if she expresses an interest in a new hat. If she mentions a ball, they tell her to dance with the laundry.[40]

Not all commercial education students were daughters of working class people however, The Boston WEIU research on *The Public Schools and Office Work* published in 1914 reported that 33 per cent of the young women surveyed were the daughters of business and professional men.[41] Given the increases in young women enrolling in commercial courses in public schools after 1914 – by 1922 2,155,000 students were enrolled in business courses in public high schools, the majority of whom were young women – it makes sense that the number who were middle class and well educated increased over time.[42]

Secretarial work was included in a series of lectures on occupations for the college woman advertised in a 1916 *Vocational Guidance Bulletin*. 'Does a college trained woman make the best secretary', and 'Desirability of field for college girls', were topics included in the lecture on the profession of secretarial work.[43] Secretarial work was encouraged by collegiate educators such as Miss Beatrice Doerschuk, of Sarah Lawrence College who wrote *The Woman Secretary*, and the women who ran occupational bureaus such as the NYCBVI (New York City Bureau of Vocational Information) and the CCBO (Chicago Collegiate Bureau of Occupations), and there is some indication that recruitment was successful.[44] Twelve per cent of office workers surveyed by the BPWA (Business and Professional Women's Association) in 1922 were college graduates or had had some college work.[45]

The Attraction of Commercial Education

It is important to understand why young women of all social classes and backgrounds were attracted to commercial education in schools and why so many aspired to be stenographers. One important point is that most young women expected to get married and wanted to marry men who were suitable. The attraction of offices as marriage markets is revealed in the comments of a young woman contemplating her career in the late 1920s. Marguerite said, 'I want to get married some time. If I'm a teacher I'll never meet any men and so what is there to do except be a stenographer'. According to the person interviewing Marguerite, '... her friends ... were all stenographers who hoped to become executive secretaries and marry the boss, or failing in this, to some lesser male members of the office force'.[46] Offices clearly offered the promise of a pool of marriageable candidates and, if not that, a social circle of office mates.

It can be argued that while office workers could be compared to factory workers given the specialization of tasks and close supervision, office work offered a ladder of opportunity and a variety of workplaces from which to choose that factories did not. As Coyle put it, 'The hope of advancement has always been one of the cherished possessions of the clerical group'.[47] The perceived social and economic distance between the lower and higher rungs of the office work ladder was aptly described by WEIU researchers:

> The women who work in offices represent a wide variation of education, ability and earning capacity. At one extreme is the secretary with a college education who may have supervision over a large office and many subordinates; who can carry on the business and decide many perplexing questions in the absence of her employer and receive a yearly salary of $1,000 and $2,000. At the other extreme is the girl or woman with only a grammar school education who folds circulars or addresses envelopes in a small dingy office at one dollar or less a day or for only a few days at a time.[48]

In addition to a variety of positions, and a variety of jobs to be done, there were an enormous variety of offices to work in. Medical offices, lawyers, large corporations, stores, and factories all maintained office staffs that were increasingly run by women, and although most young women may have occupied the low level clerical jobs that were not highly paid, there were also women in well-paid secretarial positions. Moreover, these secretaries were close to the power figures in the organization, owners and managers. Given the structure of the work force during the Progressive Era, it was not realistic for the average young woman to aspire to be the president of a corporation, such as the enterprise run by the mythical 'Daddy Warbucks'. It was realistic, however, to aspire to be Grace Farrell, Daddy Warbuck's secretary. High school commercial courses were the path to that dream.

In summary, commercial education's success was based on a number of considerations. Students who were trained for office work could look forward to the possibility of moving up the job ladder, even as the ladder got longer. Social mobility was possible by virtue of exposure to eligible men. Employers benefited from the training offered by public schools. Administrators appreciated the high enrollments in their commercial classes and parents who could afford to keep their daughters in school were pleased with a vocational course that provided tangible benefits. Thus, regardless of the female ghetto they helped to create, commercial programs were the most successful vocational education programs to emerge from that era and they were the product of client preferences rather than instrumentality on the part of vocational educators.

What also seems important about commercial education is that programs did not begin as sorting devices for young women based on gender and class, even though they ended up that way. The cultural myth/reality of female dependence on male authority and guidance was replicated in offices and commercial education programs as an unquestioned component of the workplace. Neither middle class nor working class women were willing to dispose of the boundaries of their female spheres, but they needed to negotiate them. Concurrent and related to the development of a white collar ghetto and then a pink collar ghetto in offices, was the shaping and mediating of economic realities by gender, ethnic, and class-based expectations.

Notes

1 Latimer, J.F. (1958) *What's Happened to Our High Schools*, Washington, DC, Public Affairs Press, p. 36.
2 Malot, J.O. (1928) 'Commercial Education', USBE (United States Bureau of Education), *Biennial Survey of Education, 1924–1926*, Bulletin 1928, No. 25 Washington, DC, GPO (Government Printing Office), p. 252.
3 Commercial high schools were located in Boston, Worcester and Springfield MA, Brooklyn NY, Washington, DC, Atlanta GA, Pittsburgh PA, Columbus and Cleveland OH, Omaha NE, San Francisco CA, and Portland OR, see USBE (1919) 'Business Education in Secondary Schools', Bulletin No. 55, Washington, DC, GPO, p. 12.
4 Weiss, J. *Education for Clerical Work: a History of Commercial Education in the US since 1850*, Chapter 2, 'The Nineteenth-century Private Commercial School', and Chapter 3, 'Commercial Education Comes to the High School: the Popularization of Public Secondary Education'; WEIU (Women's Educational and Industrial Union), Department of Research, (1914) *The Public Schools and Women in*

Office Service, Boston, WEIU, pp. 5–11; Woody, T. (1966) *Women's Education in the United States*, New York, Octagon Press, 2, pp. 66–69.

5 Evans, M. (1924) 'The Status of Secondary Commercial Education', *Vocational Education Magazine*, April, p. 645.

6 Counts, G. (1926) *The Senior High School Curriculum*, Chicago, The University of Chicago, published in conjunction with *The School Review and The Elementary School Journal*, p. 92.

7 Patty, W.W. (1920) 'Opportunities for Vocational Education in California Evening High Schools', unpublished Master's thesis, University of California, Berkeley, pp. 29–31.

8 Broadwell, G.L. (1923) 'The Functions of the Co-ordinator For Girls in Part-time Education', Master's thesis, University of California, Berkeley, p. 28; Coole, R.M. (1937) 'A Comparison of Anglo American and Latin-American Girls in Grades V–XI With Reference to Their Vocational and Academic and Recreational Preferences and Aversions', unpublished Master's thesis, University of Texas, Austin, pp. 11–16; Van Denburg, J.K. (1911) *Causes of the Elimination of Students in Public Secondary Schools of New York City*, New York, Teachers' College, Columbia University, p. 57; Franklin, E.E. (1924) *The Permanency of Interests of Junior High School Pupils*, Baltimore, Johns Hopkins University Press, p. 35; Ripley, C.A. (1931) 'A Study of Homemaking Education in San Jose High School', Master's thesis, Stanford University; USBE (1917) 'The Public School System of San Francisco, California', *United States Bureau of Education Bulletin 1917, No. 46*, Washington, DC, GPO, p. 516.

9 F.V. Thompson, Assistant Superintendent of Boston Schools and A. Roncovieri, Superintendent of San Francisco Schools are examples of what D. Tyack and E. Hansot call 'administrative progressives', in that they were administrators who identified themselves with business interests. See Tyack, D. and Hansot, E. (1982) *Managers of Virtue, Public School Leadership in America, 1820–1980*, New York, Basic Books, Inc., p. 106; Weiss, J. 'Education for Clerical Work', p. 133.

10 Roncovieri, A. (1916) *Report of the Superintendent of Schools of San Francisco, California for the Fiscal Year Ending June 30, 1916*, San Francisco, p. 901.

11 Barnhart, E.W. (1923) 'Commercial Occupations in the Census Reports', *Vocational Education Magazine*, October, p. 117.

12 USBE (1919) 'Business Education in Secondary Schools', 55, p. 15; see also Mikesele, W.B. (1924) 'Wherein are High School Commercial Courses Inadequate', *Vocational Education Magazine*, February, p. 640; Thompson, F.V. (1917) 'The Senior High School: Its Function and Organization', NSPIE (National Society for the Promotion of Industrial Education) *Bulletin No. 24, Proceedings Tenth Annual Meeting, Indianapolis, February 21–24, 1917*, New York, NSPIE, p. 183.

13 Thompson, F.V. 'Commercial Education', *RCE 1915*, 1, Chapter 10, pp. 279–293 cited in Weiss, J. 'Education for Clerical Work'.

14 Leake, A.H. (1918) *The Vocational Education of Girls and Women*, New York, Macmillan Company, p. 369; (1919) 'Retail Selling Teacher-Training Courses to be Given by New York University', *The Vocational Summary*, 1, 11, March, p. 20; (1914) 'Of Current Interest', *Manual Training and Vocational Education Magazine*, p. 186; San Francisco Board of Education, Unpublished minutes of board meeting, 11 July 1916 notes that Marshall Hale, on behalf of the San Francisco Retail Dry Goods association, requested information as to whether any appropriation had been made for industrial training in salesmanship; Young, F.T. (1922) 'Retail Education in the Stores', *Vocational Education Magazine*, October, p. 106.

15 Leake, A.H. *The Vocational Education of Girls and Women*, p. 369; (1914) 'Of

Current Interest', *Manual Training and Vocational Education Magazine*, p. 186; (1923) 'News Notes', *Vocational Education Magazine*, December, p. vi.

16 Malot, J.O. 'Commercial Education', USBE *Biennial Survey of Education, 1926–1928*, p. 248.

17 *Retail Selling Teacher Training*, p. 20.

18 FBVE (Federal Board of Vocational Education) (1921) *Fifth Annual Report to Congress of the Federal Board for Vocational Education*, Washington, DC, GPO, pp. 89–93; FBVE, (1918) *Retail Selling*, Bulletin No. 22, Washington, DC, GPO, throughout; see also Norton, H.R., USBE (1917) 'Department Store Education', *Bulletin 1917, No. 9*, Washington, DC, GPO.

19 In New York City, in 1917 there were fifty students in salesmanship classes which were offered to part-time coop students. The report summary found that salesmanship programs 'have not been entirely satisfactory'. Not only were enrollments very low, but the classes were dominated by young women, contrary to their original purpose of drawing young men into commercial education classes. (1918) *New York City Industrial Education Survey*, New York, Manhattan Linotype, Co. Printers, pp. 183–186.

20 Leake, A. (1911) *The Vocational Education ...*, pp. 363–368; Prince, L.W. 'What the Schools can do to Train for Work in Department Stores', NSPIE *Bulletin No. 13, Proceedings of the Fourth Annual Convention*, New York, NSPIE, pp. 17–19.

21 *US Women at Work 1870–1930*, Ann Arbor, UMI Press, p. 36. Rotella, E.J. (1933) *From Home to Office*, Breckenridge, S.P. *Women in the Twentieth Century*, New York, McGraw Hill Book Co., p. 174.

22 Butler, E.B. (1912) *Saleswomen in Mercantile Stores*, New York, Russell Sage, p. 22; Donovan, F. (1974) *The Saleslady*, New York, Arno Press, reprint of 1929 edition; The 'Sexy Saleslady' is the title of a chapter in Ryan, M.P. (1975) *Womanhood in America from Colonial Times to the Present*, New York, New Viewpoints, p. 251; Higashi, S. (1979) 'Cinderella vs Statistics: the Silent Movie Heroine as the Jazz Age Working Girl', in Kelley, M. (Ed.) *Woman's Being, Woman's Place*, Boston, G.K. Hall & Co., pp. 111–114.

23 Funding was provided for part-time students who were employed, but full funding was not made available until 1963. See FBVE (1919) *Commercial Education, Organization and Administration*, Bulletin No. 34, Washington, DC, GPO, p. 7; Healy, R. and Lund, D.(1975) 'Massachusetts Law, Women and Vocational Education: Final Report', *Organization for Social and Technical Innovation*, Lincoln, ERIC ed. 114598, p. 63.

24 Norton, T.L. (1939) *Education for Work*, New York, McGraw Hill, p. 40 cited in Weiss, J. 'Educating for Clerical Work', p. 217.

25 On the feminization of clerical workers see Davies, M. (1982) *Woman's Place is at the Typewriter*, Philadelphia, Temple University Press, pp. 51–78; Jackson, N. and Gaskell, J. (1987) 'White Collar Vocationalism: The Rise of Commercial Education in Ontario and British Columbia 1870–1920', *Curriculum Inquiry*, 117.

26 Counts, G. (1926) *The Senior High School Curriculum*, Chicago, The University of Chicago Press, pp. 93–95.

27 FBVE (1931) *Fifteenth Annual Report to Congress, 1931*, Washington, DC, GPO, p. 54.

28 McKeever, W.A. (1912) *Farm Boys and Girls*, New York, Macmillan Co., p. 294.

29 WEIU, *The Public Schools and Women in Office Service*, p. 155; Ware, C. (1935) *Greenwich Village 1920–1930*, Boston, Houghton Mifflin Company, p. 68.

30 Coole, R.M. 'A Comparison of Anglo American and Latin American Girls in Grades V–XI With Reference to Their Vocational Academic and Recreational Preferences and Aversions', p. 37; Clark, M. (1936) 'A Preliminary Survey of the Employment Possibilities of Spanish American Girls Receiving Commercial

Training in San Antonio Secondary Schools', unpublished Master's thesis, University of Texas, pp. 29–72.

31 There were 8,138 black women in clerical work in 1920, according to census statistics. This number amounted to approximately 1 per cent of the entire clerical work force. Of these women, 1,955 were stenographers and typists, which amounted to .003 per cent of all stenographers and typists. Black women were hampered both by discrimination in the workplace and by lack of facilities for training in the few extant black high schools; 2 per cent of all black high students were enrolled in commercial courses in 1925. According to E. Krug, 'thousands of black youth' in Southern States had no public high school to attend. On black clerical workers see Hill, J. (1923 reprint 1978) *Women in Gainful Occupations 1870–1920*, Washington, DC, GPO, 1923 Census Monograph, reprint in Westport, Greenwood Press, pp. 186–187; on blacks in high schools see Krug, E. (1972) *The Shaping of the American High School Vol. 2, 1920–1941*, Madison, University of Wisconsin Press, p. 126; on black women in the workplace see Jones, J. (1985) *Labor of Love, Labor of Sorrow, Black Women, Work and the Family from Slavery to the Present*, New York, Basic Books Inc, pp. 178–181; Weiss, J. 'Education for Clerical Work: A History of Commercial Education in the United States Since 1850', p. 233.

32 GFWC (General Federation of Women's Clubs), (1913) *The Federation Bulletin*, August, p. 11.

33 GFWC (1913) *Federation Bulletin*, August, p. 11.

34 WEIU, *The Public Schools and Women in Office Service*, p. 25.

35 Counts, G. (1922) *The Selective Character of American Education*, Chicago, University of Chicago Press, p. 57, cited in Weiss, J. 'Education for Clerical Work: A History of Commercial Education in the United States Since 1850', p. 175.

36 Lynd, R.S. and Lynd, H.M. (1929 reprinted 1956) *Middletown, A Study in Modern American Culture*, New York, Harcourt Brace and World Inc., p. 49.

37 Coyle, G. (1929 reprinted in 1974) 'Women in Clerical Occupations', *Women in the Modern World, The Annals*, Philadelphia, The American Academy of Political and Social Science, 142, reprinted in New York, Arno Press, p. 181; Hutchins, G. (1934) *Women Who Work*, New York, International Publishers, p. 83.

38 Manning, C. (1930 reprinted 1970) *The Immigrant Woman and Her Job*, New York, Arno Press and the New York Times, reprint of the US Department of Labor, Bulletin of the Women's Bureau, No. 74, Washington, DC, GPO, p. 59; Ware, C. *Greenwich Village ...*, p. 69; Wilson, M.G. (1979) *The American Woman in Transition, The Urban Influence, 1870–1920*, Westport, Greenwood Press, pp. 117–119.

39 Coole, R.M. 'A Comparison of Anglo American and Latin American Girls in Grades V–XI with Reference to Their Vocational Academic and Recreational Preferences and Aversions', p. 55.

40 Howe, I. and Libo, K. (Eds) (1979) *How We Lived, A Documentary History of Immigrant Jews in America, 1800–1930*, [quoting 'Forward', 8/8/05] New York, New American Library, p. 139.

41 WEIU, *The Public Schools and Women in Office Service*, p. 163.

42 Latimer, J. *What's Happened to Our High Schools*, pp. 69, 145.

43 (1916) *Vocational Guidance Bulletin*, II, No. 6, June/July 1916, p. 3 in Papers of the NYCBVI (New York City Bureau of Vocational Information) B-3, Box 17, Folder 226, Schlesinger Library, Radcliffe College.

44 See letter from B. Doerschuk to Mrs R. Borden dated 7 May 1953 in Papers of the NYCBVI B-3, Manuscript Inventory; see also 'Women in Industry', lecture IV, 'Office work as training for executive positions', by Miss Eleanor Gilbert, Box 1, Folder 7, Papers of the NYCBVI, Schlesinger Library, Radcliffe College.

45 Elliott, M. and Manson, G. 'Some Factors Affecting Earnings of Business and Professional Women', *Women in the Modern World*, pp. 137, 143.
46 Donovan, F.R. (1929 reprinted 1974) *The Saleslady*, New York, Arno Press, reprint by Chicago, The University of Chicago Press, p. 1.
47 Coyle, G. *Women in Clerical Occupations*, p. 185.
48 WEIU, *Public Schools and Women in Office Service*, p. 2.

Part 3   Conclusions

Gender, interacting with race, ethnicity and class was a theme in variation in schools. What was possible and what was not possible were profoundly influenced by female role expectations. Program adoption was accomplished in concert with role definitions and labor market sanctions. Yet as this section has demonstrated students and parents voted with their presence in vocational programs. Serious trade education, such as was conceptualized by the National Women's Trade Union League, was not congruent with sex role norms; administrators did not adopt it and students did not lobby for its adoption. Home economics and clerical education were both appropriate interests for students and thus they were adopted into school curricula. Once there, home economics was virtually ignored while clerical education was an enrollment success.

Using gender as a wash on the canvas, there were three other factors that differentially influenced both the adoption of curriculum and student response; they were politics, economics and ideology. In the area of politics home economics stands out as the most profoundly affected program. A main factor in the almost universal incorporation of home economics into the curriculum was support from educators and interest groups. The General Federation of Women's Clubs, rural life advocates and supporters, family protection groups such as the Society for the Prevention of Infant Mortality and the American Home Economics Association were effective in lobbying for expanded programs in public schools prior to the passage of federal legislation. Following the passage of the Smith-Hughes legislation in 1917, the AHEA worked in close cooperation with the National Education Association and the National Society for the Promotion of Industrial Education to lobby for funds, facilities and supervisory personnel at all levels of public education systems. As indicated in Chapter 7 they achieved remarkable success in erecting and sustaining the home economics bureaucracy.

In contrast to home economics, the trade education lobby, suffered from its lack of political connections. The National Women's Trade Union League was powerful enough to engineer the appointment of one of their representatives to the federal commission, however they were not well connected in education. They did not lobby for representation in the National Education Association and were not found presenting at national or state meetings the way the home economics lobby was. They occasionally worked with the National Society for

Promotion of Industrial Education, which became an active supporter of home economics following the passage of Smith-Hughes, but generally chose to lobby in select urban areas for trade education. The San Francisco Board of Education minutes, for example, contain a letter from the NWTUL regarding trade education; and one of its celebrated coups was the glove making course adopted by the Chicago School System. Despite occasional local victories, and its representation on the National Commission, it was not a highly visible or influential force in the education community. The politics of commercial education had little effect on its success although tension between interest groups did affect federal funding and the extent to which business education aligned itself with the vocational education community. Far more important than interest groups politics over image and identity were economic issues; in 1900 4.5 per cent of the female labor force was in clerical work and in 1930 that figure had grown to 18.8 per cent.[1] The consistently growing need for office workers, combined with the social appeal of white collar work made it highly desirable.

Trade education and home economics were both hampered in their appeal to students by economic factors. Home economics led to a limited number of occupations and in fact was regarded as training for nongainful employment or homemaking. There was no appeal of potential remuneration, except for the young women who were training for home economics teaching or perhaps institutional home economics. This was a critical factor in the failure of home economics because young women and their parents invested in high school for economic and social return; home economics yielded neither.

Trade education, on the other hand, was hampered economically in two ways. First, the feminine industries – dressmaking and millinery – were shrinking and could not absorb all the young women who were potential trade education students. Second, expansion into traditional male areas of trade education was firmly opposed by unions, and most male employers. This last point is significant because it speaks to the fact that men were willing to hire women as cheap labor under some circumstances such as in offices or under emergency conditions such as war, however when normal peace-time conditions were restored, employers eschewed the presence of women in their factories and industries except in the low paying unskilled and semiskilled work. Whereas women were welcomed in offices formerly considered unfit for women, they were consistently excluded from blue collar work outside the areas carefully designated as women's work. Compounding this reality about trade education was the fact that parents wanted their offspring to do better than they had done. For many of them who worked long hours at tedious, excessively grueling, or dirty work, a factory was not a desirable place for their children to work.

Apart from the factors that influenced the success or failure of particular programs, there are some generalizations that emerge from the study of practice. One is that neither schools, nor students were easily diverted from their agendas. Thus the home economics lobby was successful in influencing administrators to adopt home economics, and administrators were amenable because they saw it as within the scope of their responsibilities to provide some education for homemaking. However, administrators were not willing to alter dramatically the academic agenda of high school. Most were not willing to require high school courses in home economics and most did not lend their full support to developing the exemplary curriculum that home economists and progressive reformers envisioned.

Similarly, students and parents had their agendas and they were not easily diverted or shortchanged. The parents who could invest in a high school education for their daughter wanted a good job as a result, both for the years immediately following high school when they were likely to be living at home and participating in a family economy and in the event of bad luck following marriage. They also wanted their daughters to meet 'nice people', and specifically to meet nice young men to marry. Thus most parents did not encourage their daughters to take up trade education nor did they lobby for expanded definitions of trade education; but instead they encouraged them either to take commercial education which led to office work, or general course work which would lead to teaching. Attempts to subvert student and parent goals did not work. As a General Federation of Women's Club member observed about young black women in commercial education, they might not have any chance of getting a job, but these days it would not be a good idea to suggest that they take domestic science instead.[2]

It is evident that schools mirrored the delicate power relationships in society generally. Complex forces were brought to bear on curriculum decisions for young women. Interest group politics, economic concerns, and social forces were all woven into the pattern of vocational schooling for young women. Yet as stated before, the issue of gender and woman's place in society was the over-riding theme.

Notes

1 Rotella, E. (1981) *From Home to Office, US Women at Work 1870–1930*, Ann Arbor, UMI Press, Table 2.12.
2 GFWC (1913) *Federation Bulletin*, p. 11.

11   Meanings

By 1930 vocational curricula had been funded by the federal government for more than ten years, and vocational programs were entrenched in the secondary school curriculum. The vocational function of schools was embedded in the fabric of course work, and the fabric was shaded symbolically in pink and blue. Vocational courses for young women consisted of training for office work, home economics, and some trade education which for the most part was in the needle trades. The seemingly predictable outcome, segregation on the basis of gender, belies the complex history of the movement.

As I have argued in this book there was a constellation of social, economic, and political forces that converged on the vocational education movement for young women in the Progressive Era. The crux of the issue was not simply what programs and courses would be offered in vocational education programs for females, but how their own vocational options would be defined by women from different racial, ethnic, and class backgrounds. Women's vocational education was thus thrust into a much larger discussion, and the valance attached to positions adopted and decisions made was significantly enhanced. Female institution building that developed in the nineteenth century was carried over in the twentieth century by women who saw themselves as the instruments of change and the seat of decision making. Building on that immediate legacy, advocates of vocational training for young women placed women at the center of significant social and economic change and linked societal change to home economics and preparation for women's trades. Home economics moved beyond rhetoric into the curricula of schools around the United States, and it became a standard offering in most junior and senior high schools.

Yet, as part of a broad vision to reform society and a more narrow vision to shore up homemaking and women's separate sphere in it, the home economics movement was apparently unsuccessful. While the 'new woman' of the twenties embraced marriage, the ideal of municipal housekeeping and the passionate rhetoric that accompanied it ebbed away, leaving secondary schools with three important legacies. The first was the department of home economics which never managed to lift itself above plain sewing and cooking into the hybrid home economics envisioned by the foremothers of the movement.

The second, identified by Rutherford in her thesis, *Feminism and the Secondary School Curriculum* was the impact of home economics on the participation of

Table 11.1: *Percentage of girls in mathematics and science courses in the last four years of public high schools[2]*

	1900	1928
Chemistry	55	42
Geology	59	43
Algebra	58	47
Trigonometry	47	22
Physics	57	34

women in science and mathematics courses.[1] As the reader will recall, home economists lobbied for practical science and mathematics curricula, such as domestic chemistry and home physics. While the evidence indicates that feminized science and math courses were infrequently adopted, young women's enrollment in mathematics and science courses dropped after 1900.

According to Rutherford, social support for girls to enroll in advanced algebra, trigonometry or sciences was absent after the beginning of the twentieth century. This was attributed to the impact of domesticated sciences on the secondary curriculum.

The third legacy – the most elusive and potentially the most significant – is the general understanding and expectation that men and women will pursue different occupations and professions and that the school's role is to counsel and educate young people for that expectation. Prior to the vocational training movement, women's curriculum in secondary schools closely resembled young men's, and after the advent of the vocational movement women held a separate place in the curriculum, symbolically and in the physical space of both home economics and commercial education. Sex segregation in secondary schools was thus a specific result of the vocational movement.

A counter argument would point out that schools were vocationalized by virtue of teaching and commercial work before the turn of the century and that sex segregation was already an operative reality when schools became explicitly vocational after 1900. While the latter argument is accurate it ignores the power of the rhetoric or myth to shape the way people view their world and themselves. The vocational education movement was a forum for discussions and ultimately decisions about a woman's place in the world. The necessary decisions resulted in the validation of the social myth that a woman's place is in the home and that a woman's place in the work world is marginal. Elizabeth Janeway has pointed out, that social myths exist quite apart from reality; thus even though home economics classes went begging for students and commercial classes overflowed, sex segregation as an ideology was institutionalized.[3]

Social myths can and do influence behavior, even though they may be contradictory to behavior. Commercial education in secondary schools was an example of a course of study that in its formative years contradicted the social myth of sex segregation while at the same time it was influenced by it. Susan Carter and Catherine Poss can be credited with work that occasioned a re-examination of the relevance of secondary schooling for young women. They have argued that young women dominated high school enrollments because schools were vocationally relevant. In fact Carter argues, they were more vocationally relevant for young women than for young men because they offered training for teaching and commercial work.[4] Young women in rural and urban areas all over the United States flocked to commercial courses in hopes of landing an office job. The fact that schools were training young women for paid labor did not cause any overt conflict with the prevailing ideology that a woman's place was in the home, even though there was an inherent contradiction. A number of historians have pointed out the flexible nature of our role prescriptions when there is a pressing labor market need. As Carolyn Ware bluntly puts it, 'Industry has always accepted and used women when it has needed them'.[5] In the case of commercial education in schools, the role prescriptions were either flexed – so that offices were likened to homes and secretaries to wives away from home – or ignored in response to a receptive labor market.

What did cause a conflict, however, was the fact that young men and young women were being trained for the same positions. Women sat alongside young men in commercial classes through the 1920s, often training for similar jobs: 20.9 per cent of all male high school students were enrolled in bookkeeping in 1928, along with 47.0 per cent of all female students. Many vocational educators were disturbed about the fact that boys and girls were taking the same courses.[6] The power of the prescription or the social myth that men and women must hold different positions helped shape commercial education and the role that women assumed in the clerical sector of the job market. As Margery Davies convincingly argued, clerical work was steadily feminized in spite of what vocational educators would have preferred, and the major contradictions that existed between ideology and practice in the first decades of the century were eliminated.[7] Clerical work was rationalized as women's work such that commercial education became a feminine ghetto in schools. The population of the ghetto is now both feminine and working class according to Linda Valli's research on cooperative education.[8]

Trade education, I would argue, was never acceptable for women, and the social myth that women do not belong in industrial work has been continually invoked regardless of the reality. Vocational educators in state and local bureaucracies would not accept programs for women's blue collar work in schools, and parents and students did not pressure schools for it. The unreceptive labor market was a significant factor in women's participation in blue collar work, and women who lobbied for trade education were sensitive to the constraints imposed by it. It seems very plausible that women such as Mary Schenck Woolman who were strong supporters of women in industry confined the role to feminine industries and supported a conservative definition of trade education because it was more likely to gain acceptance than a more liberal expanded definition. Margaret Rossiter suggests in her work on *Women Scientists in America*, that when women were unable to make gains using arguments about equity, the conservatives among them moved in to stress women's special skills, and that between the two strategies, women were able to mine all the available niches for women.[9] In any case, barriers to trade education, both in terms of social myth and the reality of the job market were and continue to be effective, while the feminine 'niches' are still extant.

The rhetoric and the reality of vocational training for young women in the progressive era interacted to create a relatively complex pattern. Social prescription labor market constraints in blue collar work, labor market sanctions in clerical work, students' aspirations, and parental ambitions combined with progressive-era reformism to yield a relatively narrow range of offerings: clerical work, home economics, and trade education. Yet few people were concerned about these limited offerings. Schools, educators, and the women who shaped the programs saw to it that vocational training included the necessary cultural prescriptions and the practical courses lead to jobs that parents supported and to which their daughters aspired. It was not until the second wave of feminism that the assumptions which were so explicit in discussion at the turn of the century were resurrected for re-examination.

In terms of the revisionist project, this history of the women's vocational education movement both confirms and challenges arguments of social and economic reproduction. Kantor concludes in *Learning to Earn* that the conceptual linking of school to paid work is a significant legacy of the vocational education movement.[10] For young women the connections are elusive – now you see it and now you don't. Since women's work has not been viewed as real work in terms of contribution to the gross national product or industrial productivity it could not be invited in as the centerpiece of revisionist analyses of school/work connections. Yet, both in terms of social ideology – gender role maintenance – and skills and knowledge that convert into paid work, the vocational education movement and its legacy have been very relevant for women.

This book argues that the relevance needs to be acknowledged and analyzed at a number of levels. It is clear that gender differentiation is a powerful dimension of experience in secondary schools, both historically and in a contemporary sense. But the form it takes, as S. Rosaldo argued in her early work on sex roles from a cross cultural perspective, is so variable that the context has to be identified for the generality to have meaning.[11]

The epilogue to this chapter in women's vocational education history suggests that the power of social prescription and the role of schools as both cultural transmitters, and mediators in the relationship between women, work, and families has continued to confine vocational offerings for young women. Congressional hearings on vocational legislation in the early 1960s mirrored prescriptive comments on the dual roles of women from the Progressive Era. Representative Pucinski argued for teaching young women 'the basic structure of home economics and at the same time ... a vocational skill so that when she becomes an adult if fate should cast her in the role of bread-winner as well as homemaker she will be prepared for that'.[12] When asked to elaborate, Pucinski added, 'What I was suggesting was that when we teach a young lady how to sew a hem in her dress it is just as easy to teach her how to use a power machine so if she has to get a job in a dress factory she is not going to be a stranger and she will be able to move right into that job ...'.[13] Home economics was accorded a strong vote of confidence in the 1960 legislation, along with clerical education which qualified for federal assistance for the first time.

Title IX of the Education Amendments of 1972 which prohibits sex discrimination in education included provisions for vocational education and the Vocational Education Act as amended in 1976 included provisions for eliminating sex bias and discrimination in vocational education, however despite recent efforts, 'sex segregation in vocational education remains high'.[14] For example, a 1983 study prepared by the Full Access and Rights to Education Coalition entitled 'Their "Proper Place",' found that twelve of New York City's vocational schools had primarily male enrollments, and that young women predominated in just five of these schools where the curriculum concentrated on 'traditionally' female occupations such as cosmetology and stenography.[15] In short, schools continue to provide vocational training constrained by the social myth of 'woman's place'.

Notes

1 Rutherford, M. (1977) 'Feminism and the Secondary School Curriculum, 1880–1920', unpublished Ph.D. dissertation, Stanford, Stanford University School of Education, p. 152.
2 Latimer, J.F. (1958) *What's Happened to Our High Schools*, Washington, DC, Public Affairs Press, Appendix C, Table 23, p. 149.
3 Janeway, E. (1971) *Man's World Woman's Place*, New York, Dell Publishing Co. Inc., p. 7.
4 Carter, S.B. and Prus, M. (1982) 'The Labor Market and the American High School Girl, 1890–1928', *Journal of Economic History*, XLII, No. 1, March, pp. 163–171; Katherine Poss, 'The Sexual Structuring of Education and Opportunity; A Study of the Preponderance of Girls in the US Public Secondary Schools 1870–1930 (unpublished dissertation proposal, Stanford University School of Education, 1981).
5 Ware, C.F. (1977) 'Introduction,' *Class, Sex and the Woman Worker*, Westport, Greenwood Press, p. 18.
6 Latimer, J.F. *What's Happened to Our High School* ..., p. 150.
7 Davies, M.W. (1982) *Woman's Place Is At the Typewriter*, Philadelphia, Temple University Press.
8 Valli, L. (1983) 'Becoming Clerical Workers: The Relations Between Office Education and the Culture of Femininity', in Apple, M. and Weis, L. (Eds) *Ideology and Practice in Schooling*, Philadelphia, Temple University Press.
9 Rosaldo, S. and Lamphere, L. (1974) *Woman, Culture and Society*, Stanford, Stanford University Press.
10 Kantor, H. (1988) *Learning to Earn*, Madison, University of Wisconsin Press.
11 Rossiter, M.W. (1982) *Women Scientists in America*, Baltimore, John Hopkins University Press, pp. xvii–xviii.
12 US Congress, House of Representatives Hearings on Vocational Education, 1963, cited in Healy, R. and Lund, D. (1975) 'Massachusetts Law, Women and Vocational Education: Final Report,' unpublished paper, Organization for Social and Technical Innovation, Lincoln, Ed. 114598, p. 71.
13 Healy, R. and Lund, D. 'Massachusetts Law, Women and ...,' p. 71.
14 Wells, J. (1983) Statement of the National Coalition for Women and Girls in Education, Washington, DC, National Coalition for Women and Girls in Education, cited in Klein, S. (Ed.) (1985) *Handbook for Achieving Sex Equity Through Education*, Baltimore, John Hopkins University Press, p. 347.
15 Purnick, J. (1983) 'Vocational Schools Are Accused of Sexual Bias,' *New York Times*, 28 January.

Plates

Plate 1:
These young women are in laundry education at the National Training School for Women and Girls in Washington, DC. This course was a special province of young African-American women.

Plate 2:
The sign in front of the building proudly advertises the mission of the program.

Plate 3:
These 'working girls' and women sat side-by-side learning dressmaking in the Free Evening Schools of Boston, Massachusetts. Dressmaking and millinery were popular courses in the evening schools. Library of Congress.

Plate 4:
These young women who look so studious are part of a home economics class in Washington, DC Schools. The board diagrams and microscope work seem to advertise the comprehensiveness of the cooking curriculum. Library of Congress.

Plate 5:
Young African-American women turned to private education for courses and programs that were not very available in public schools by virtue of discriminatory practices. This photograph of aspiring stenographers was taken at the National Training School for Girls and Women in Washington, DC around 1925. Library of Congress.

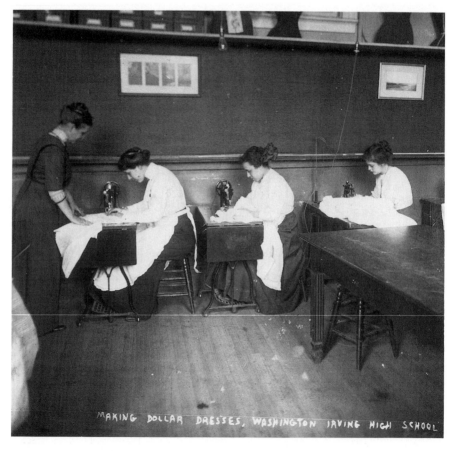

Plate 6:
Sewing classes provided young women with access to sewing machines and the opportunity to make clothes along with the obvious gender stereotyping. These young women at Washington Irving High School in New York City are making 'dollar dresses'. Library of Congress.

Index